CORE SKILLS

MW00999230

Language Arts

ISBN 13: 978-0-7398-7089-1

ISBN 10: 0-7398-7089-0

10 11 12 13 14 15 0892 12 11 10

Steck Vaughn™

A Harcourt Achieve Imprint

www.Steck-Vaughn.com
1-800-531-5015

Contents

Introduction

Core Skills: Language Arts was developed to help your child improve the language skills he or she needs to succeed. The book emphasizes skills in the key areas of

- grammar,
- punctuation,
- vocabulary,
- writing, and
- research.

The lessons included in the book provide many opportunities for your child to practice and apply important language and writing skills. These skills will help your child excel in all academic areas, increase his or her scores on standardized tests, and have a greater opportunity for success in his or her career.

About the Book

The book is divided into six units:

- Parts of Speech
- Sentences
- Mechanics
- Vocabulary and Usage
- Writing
- Research Skills

Your child can work through each unit of the book, or you can pinpoint areas for extra practice.

Lessons have specific instructions and examples and are designed for your child to complete independently. Grammar lessons range from using nouns and verbs to constructing better sentences. Writing exercises range from the friendly letter to the book report. With this practice, your child will gain extra confidence as he or she works on daily school lessons or standardized tests.

A thorough answer key is also provided to check the quality of answers.

A Step Toward Success

Practice may not always make perfect, but it is certainly a step in the right direction. The activities in *Core Skills: Language Arts* are an excellent way to ensure greater success for your child.

Nouns

A **noun** is a word that names a person, place, or thing.

The words <u>a</u>, <u>an</u>, and <u>the</u> are clues that show a noun is near.

Examples:

   a <u>man</u>, an <u>elephant</u>, the <u>yard</u>

DIRECTIONS Find the nouns, or naming words, below. Write the nouns on the lines.

WORD BOX

apple	car	eat	hear	rug	bird	chair
girl	hot	tree	boy	desk	gone	over
truck	came	dirty	grass	pen	up	tiny

1. _____

2. _____

3. _____

4. _____

5. _____

6. _____

7. _____

8. _____

9. _____

10. _____

11. _____

12. _____

DIRECTIONS Circle the two nouns in each sentence.

13. The girl eats an apple.

14. A bird flies to the tree.

15. A chair is by the desk.

16. A boy sits in the chair.

17. The girl plays with a truck.

Nouns, page 2

A word that names a person or an animal is called a noun. A word that names a place or a thing is called a noun.
Example:
    The <u>girl</u> and her <u>dog</u> sat on a <u>bench</u> in the <u>park</u>.

 Circle the noun or nouns in each sentence. You should find eleven nouns in all.

1. My sister plays in the park.

2. She rides in a car with our mother.

3. Sometimes our dog goes, too.

4. A boy feeds birds under the trees.

5. Let's go to the playground!

6. I see a cat under the slide.

 Look at the nouns you circled. Decide if each noun names a person, a place, a thing, or an animal. Write the noun in the correct space in the chart below.

Person	Place	Thing	Animal

Proper Nouns

A noun is a word that names a person, place, or thing. A **proper noun** is a word that names a special person, place, or thing. A proper noun begins with a capital letter.

Examples:

Noun	Proper Noun
girl	Kayla Stone
park	Yellowstone Park
bread	Tasty Bread

 **Find the proper nouns in the box. Write the proper nouns on the lines.**

				WORD BOX
baseball	Bob's Bikes	Bridge Road	children	
China	Elf Corn	Gabriel	Lindsey	
man	New York City	Oregon	Pat Green	
prince	robin	State Street	town	

1. _____   6. _____

2. _____   7. _____

3. _____   8. _____

4. _____   9. _____

5. _____   10. _____

 **Circle the proper noun in each sentence.**

11. I bought apples at Hill's Store.

12. The store is on Baker Street.

13. It is near Stone Library.

14. I gave an apple to Emily Fuller.

Names and Titles of People and Animals

The names of people and animals are proper nouns. The first and last names of a person or animal begin with a capital letter.

The titles of people begin with a capital letter. Most titles end with a period. These are titles of people:

Mr. Mrs. Ms. Miss Dr.

Examples:

<u>Jack Sprat</u> went to the airport.

<u>Mrs. Sprat</u> is looking for her dog <u>Fluffy</u>.

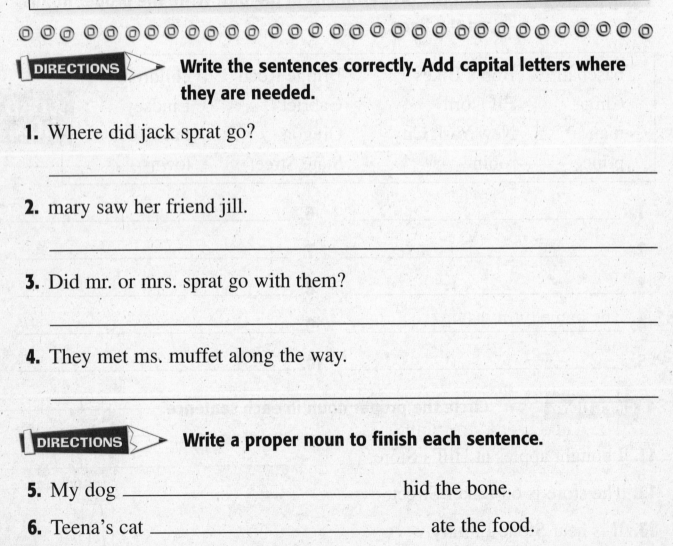

| DIRECTIONS | Write the sentences correctly. Add capital letters where they are needed. |

1. Where did jack sprat go?

_____

2. mary saw her friend jill.

_____

3. Did mr. or mrs. sprat go with them?

_____

4. They met ms. muffet along the way.

_____

| DIRECTIONS | Write a proper noun to finish each sentence. |

5. My dog _____ hid the bone.

6. Teena's cat _____ ate the food.

Names of Special Places

The names of special places are proper nouns. Cities, states, and names of streets begin with a capital letter. The names of countries also begin with a capital letter.

Examples: Jack saw his friends in <u>Miami</u>, <u>Florida</u>.
Their house is at 212 <u>Coconut Drive</u>.
I live in the <u>United States of America</u>.

DIRECTIONS ▷ **Write the sentences correctly. Add capital letters where they are needed.**

1. They walked along main street.

_____

2. My uncle drove through indiana and ohio.

_____

3. We went on a trip to mexico.

_____

DIRECTIONS ▷ **Write a proper noun to finish each sentence.**

4. The name of my state is _____.

5. The name of my town is _____.

6. The name of my street is _____.

7. The name of my school is _____.

8. _____ is a pretty place to see in our town.

Days of the Week, Months, and Holidays

> The names of the days of the week are proper nouns. They begin with capital letters.
>
> The names of the months are also proper nouns. They begin with capital letters.
>
> The names of holidays are proper nouns, too. Each important word in the name of the holiday begins with a capital letter.
>
> *Examples:*
>
> The man flew in a spaceship on <u>Saturday</u>.
>
> In <u>December,</u> he drives in the snow.
>
> He had a picnic on the <u>Fourth of July</u>.

DIRECTIONS ▷ **Complete each sentence. Use the words from the box. Find the day, month, or holiday that begins with the same letter as the underlined word.**

| Wednesday | Thanksgiving | Saturday | February | July | **WORD BOX** |

1. Francis Foley did not <u>walk</u> on _____.

2. He <u>flew</u> in _____.

3. Sometimes he <u>sails</u> on _____.

4. He <u>thinks</u> he will be home for _____.

DIRECTIONS ▷ **Write a proper noun to complete each sentence.**

5. My birthday is in _____.

6. My favorite day is _____.

7. My favorite holiday is _____.

Singular and Plural Nouns

A noun is a word that names a person, place, or thing.
A noun can tell about more than one person, place, or thing. Add <u>s</u> to most nouns to make them mean "more than one."
Examples:

One <u>girl</u> wears a black hat.
Many <u>boys</u> wear funny masks.

DIRECTIONS ▷ **Circle the correct noun to complete each sentence.**

1. Two (boy, boys) went out on Halloween.

2. A (girl, girls) walked with them.

3. She wore a black (robe, robes).

4. There were two red (star, stars) on it.

5. It also had one orange (moon, moons).

6. The children walked up to a (house, houses).

7. Then, they knocked on the (door, doors).

8. Will they ask for some (treat, treats)?

9. Then, the children saw two (cat, cats).

10. Two (dog, dogs) ran down the street.

11. An (owl, owls) hooted in the darkness.

12. Many (star, stars) were in the sky.

13. The wind blew through all the (tree, trees).

14. The children clapped their (hand, hands).

15. Then, they sang a (song, songs).

Plural Nouns

Add <u>s</u> to most nouns to make them name more than one.
Examples:
   one <u>book</u>, four <u>books</u>

DIRECTIONS **Rewrite these nouns to make them name more than one.**

1. cap _____

2. chair _____

3. girl _____

4. tree _____

5. flag _____

6. boy _____

DIRECTIONS **Make the noun in ( ) mean more than one. Write the plural noun to complete the sentence.**

7. I plant _____ in my garden.
          (seed)

8. I want to grow _____.
                    (carrot)

9. I plant some _____, too.
                   (pea)

10. My _____ help me.
          (friend)

11. They want to plant _____ , too.
                         (garden)

Nouns

More Plural Nouns

Add _es_ to nouns that end with <u>x</u>, <u>ss</u>, <u>ch</u>, or <u>sh</u>
to make them name more than one.
Examples:

one <u>fox</u>, ten <u>foxes</u>

one <u>class</u>, two <u>classes</u>

one <u>branch</u>, five <u>branches</u>

one <u>bush</u>, six <u>bushes</u>

DIRECTIONS Rewrite these nouns to make them name more than one.

1. lunch _____

2. dress _____

3. glass _____

4. dish _____

5. box _____

6. watch _____

DIRECTIONS Make the noun in ( ) mean more than one. Write the plural noun to complete the sentence.

7. Two _____ walk to the park.
(fox)

8. They sit on two _____.
(bench)

9. Their seats are only _____ apart.
(inch)

10. Then, they take out paints and _____.
(brush)

11. They paint pictures of trucks and _____.
(bus)

12. They hope to paint the _____ near the park.
(church)

Irregular Plural Nouns

Some nouns change spelling to name more than one.

Examples:

      man—men

      woman—women

      child—children

      foot—feet

      tooth—teeth

 **DIRECTIONS** ▷ **Circle the correct noun in ( ) to complete each sentence.**

1. One (woman, women) is working.

2. Many (men, man) are on horses.

3. A (child, children) is wading in the stream.

4. He has no shoes on his (feet, foot).

5. The cold water makes his (teeth, tooth) chatter.

 **DIRECTIONS** ▷ **Make the noun in ( ) mean more than one. Write the plural noun to complete the sentence.**

6. The _____ pet the dogs.
         (child)

7. The little dog has big _____.
                        (foot)

8. The big dog has little _____.
                       (tooth)

9. Those _____ feed the dogs.
         (man)

10. Those _____ walk the dogs.
         (woman)

Pronouns

A **pronoun** is a word that takes the place of one or more nouns.
Examples:

<u>The mouse and the lion</u> are friends.
<u>They</u> are friends.

The pronouns <u>I</u>, <u>we</u>, <u>he</u>, <u>she</u>, <u>it</u>, and <u>they</u> are used in the naming part of a sentence.

Examples: <u>The mouse</u> helped the lion.
<u>She</u> helped the lion.

DIRECTIONS ▷ **Read the sentences. Think of a pronoun for the underlined words. Write the pronoun on the line.**

1. <u>The mouse and I</u> live in the woods. _____

2. <u>The mouse</u> fell into the spring.
_____

3. <u>The lion</u> saw the mouse fall.
_____

4. <u>The leaf</u> landed in the water.
_____

5. <u>A hunter</u> spread a net.
_____

6. <u>The net</u> was for the lion.
_____

7. <u>The mouse and the lion</u> helped each other.
_____

8. <u>The mouse and I</u> will always be friends.
_____

9. <u>The mouse and the lion</u> are happy.
_____

10. <u>The mouse and I</u> will watch out for the hunter.
_____

Using I or Me

The word <u>I</u> is always used in the naming part of a sentence.
<u>I</u> is always written with a capital letter.
Example:

    <u>I</u> go to school.

When you speak of or write about another person and yourself, always name yourself last.
Example:

    Tina and <u>I</u> are in the same class.

The word <u>me</u> follows a verb, or action word.
Examples:

    Tina makes <u>me</u> laugh.
    The teacher tells Tina and <u>me</u> to be quiet.

DIRECTIONS Write <u>I</u> or <u>me</u> to complete each sentence correctly.

1. _____ am taking a test.

2. The teacher tells _____ to stop laughing.

3. Mother takes _____ home.

4. _____ have fun with Tina.

 **DIRECTIONS** Read the sentences. Circle the correct words in ( ) to complete each sentence.

5. (Susan and I, I and Susan) are friends.

6. The teacher tells (Tina and me, me and Tina) to hush.

7. (I and Tina, Tina and I) eat lunch together.

8. Mr. Smith asks (Susan and me, Susan and I) to pass out the papers.

Action Verbs

An **action verb** is a word that shows action. Verbs tell what a person, place, or thing does.
Examples:

      People <u>drive</u> across the country.
      We <u>walk</u> to school.

 **Circle the verb in each sentence.**

1. Eric runs by Mr. and Mrs. Wilson's house.

2. He kicks a football into the air.

3. The ball breaks the Wilsons' window.

4. Mrs. Wilson looks out the door.

5. Mr. Wilson shakes his head.

6. Eric's face turns red.

7. Eric runs inside his house.

8. Mother talks to Eric about the window.

9. Mother sends Eric to the Wilsons' house.

10. Eric pays for the window.

 **Draw a line from each noun to the correct action verb.**

Nouns	Verbs
11. The boy	hops.
12. The baby	sing.
13. The rabbit	bark.
14. The birds	cries.
15. The dogs	reads.

Singular Verbs

Add <u>s</u> to an action verb that tells about one person or thing.
Examples:
The pirate <u>walks</u> quickly.
He <u>sees</u> his friends.

 DIRECTIONS **Read the sentences. Circle the correct verb in ( ) to complete each sentence.**

1. The cat (skip, skips) down the steps.

2. Two cats (play, plays) on the stairs.

3. The children (hug, hugs) the cat.

4. The cat (purr, purrs) happily.

5. A puppy (bark, barks) at the cat.

6. The boys (hide, hides) from the girls.

7. An ape (wave, waves) to them.

8. The wind (blow, blows) the trees.

9. My shadow (follow, follows) me.

10. A girl (see, sees) a shadow.

11. Mary (hear, hears) the tree speak.

12. The branches (move, moves) in the wind.

13. An owl (hoot, hoots) in the tree.

14. The children (take, takes) their treats home.

15. They (eat, eats) some fruit.

Helping Verbs

A **helping verb** works with the main verb to show action.
Use <u>has</u>, <u>have</u>, and <u>had</u> with other verbs to show action that happened in the past.
Examples:

  Chen <u>has</u> worked hard.
  Brit and Katie <u>have</u> helped.
  They <u>had</u> stopped earlier for a snack.

> **DIRECTIONS** > Circle the helping verb in each sentence.

1. Now we have arrived at the camp.

2. Tom and Bill have unloaded the car.

3. Mr. Green had shopped for food the day before.

4. Bob has gathered firewood.

5. Something strange has happened.

6. A spaceship has landed nearby!

> **DIRECTIONS** > Circle the correct helping verb in ( ) to complete each sentence.

7. We (has, have) built a new playground.

8. Mom and Dad (had, has) sawed the boards before.

9. Donna (has, have) sanded the wood.

10. They (has, have) painted the fence.

11. My brother and I (has, have) raked the leaves.

12. But my mother (had, have) forgotten the leaf bags.

Verbs That Do Not Show Action

Some verbs do not show action. They tell about being.

Examples:

A snake <u>is</u> a reptile.

The snake <u>was</u> hungry.

Use <u>am</u> or <u>was</u> with the word <u>I</u>.

Examples:

I <u>am</u> in the tree.

I <u>was</u> under the tree.

Use <u>is</u> or <u>was</u> with one person or thing. Use <u>are</u> or <u>were</u> with more than one person or thing.

Examples:

A lizard <u>is</u> in my garden.

Two turtles <u>were</u> in a box.

 **DIRECTIONS** **Read the sentences. Circle the correct verb in ( ) to complete each sentence.**

1. Reptiles (are, is) cold-blooded animals.

2. Some snakes (are, is) dangerous.

3. Many kinds of lizards (were, was) at the zoo.

4. A draco (is, am) a lizard.

5. Crocodiles (are, is) the largest reptiles.

6. The crocodiles (were, was) very noisy.

7. One lizard (is, are) in the box.

8. I (is, am) near the turtle's box.

9. The box (was, were) near the window.

10. The turtle (is, are) sleeping.

Present-Time Verbs

Present-time verbs tell about action that happens now.
Example: Max and Lisa <u>walk</u> to school.

 Add <u>s</u> to an action verb that tells about one person or thing.
Example:

 Lisa <u>walks</u> to school.

 Read the sentences. Circle the correct verb in ( ) to complete each sentence.

1. Max (play, plays) baseball.

2. He (run, runs) fast.

3. The girls (dance, dances) to the music.

4. Some friends (wait, waits) for Max.

5. Lisa (leap, leaps) across the floor.

 Finish the story. Add action verbs. You may use words from the box.

| sits | stands | asks | takes | walks | dances | **WORD BOX** |

Max _____ his sister to her dancing class.
He _____ on a chair to watch. The teacher
_____ him to join the class. First, he
_____ with a girl. Then, he _____
by a wall. Last, he _____ home.

Past-Time Verbs

Verbs can tell about actions in the past. Form the past tense of most verbs by adding ed.
Example:
   Mary Jo <u>planted</u> vegetables yesterday.

 **Make each sentence tell about the past. Circle the correct verb in ( ) to complete each sentence.**

1. Jeff (plays, played) with his sister.

2. The family (visited, visits) Grandmother often.

3. Mary Jo (looks, looked) out the window.

4. Then, she (jumped, jumps) up and down.

5. Grandmother (leans, leaned) back on the pillow.

6. Mary Jo (helps, helped) Grandmother.

7. Grandmother (laughs, laughed) at the baby chicks.

 **Change each sentence. Make the verb tell about the past. Write the new sentence.**

8. The girls play in the park.

_____

9. They climb over rocks.

_____

10. Their fathers call to them.

_____

Irregular Verbs

Some action verbs do not add <u>ed</u> to tell about the past.

Present	Past
go, goes	went
come, comes	came
run, runs	ran

Examples:

The boys <u>went</u> to sleep.

A dog <u>came</u> to a farm.

The raccoons <u>ran</u> into the woods.

⊚ ⊚⊚ ⊚⊚ ⊚⊚⊚ ⊚ ⊚⊚ ⊚⊚ ⊚⊚ ⊚⊚⊚ ⊚⊚ ⊚⊚ ⊚⊚⊚ ⊚⊚ ⊚⊚⊚ ⊚⊚ ⊚⊚ ⊚⊚ ⊚⊚ ⊚⊚⊚

 **Read the sentences. Circle the correct verb in ( ) to complete each sentence.**

1. Three robbers (ran, runs) out the door.

2. They (comes, came) back.

3. Four animals (goes, went) by the house.

4. The rooster and the dog (go, goes) into the kitchen.

5. The friends (run, runs) down the road.

6. A cat (goes, go) very fast.

 **Circle the verb in each sentence. Then, write each verb in the past tense.**

7. The man goes to the mill. _____

8. A donkey comes to town. _____

9. The animals come to a big house. _____

10. They run to the window. _____

Adding ed or ing to Verbs

To show that something happened in the past, add ed to most verbs.
Example:
    Don visited Liz yesterday.
To show that something is happening now, you can add ing to most verbs.
Example:
    Sue is visiting Liz now.

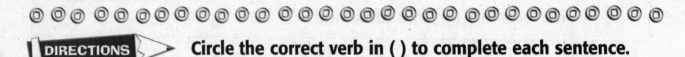

DIRECTIONS ▷ **Circle the correct verb in ( ) to complete each sentence.**

1. Terry and Joe (played, playing) basketball last week.

2. Jenna (called, calling) to them.

3. She (wanted, wanting) to play, too.

4. The boys (laughed, laughing) at her.

5. But Jenna (jumped, jumping) for the ball.

6. She (played, playing) well.

7. Terry and Joe are not (laughed, laughing) anymore.

8. Now, Jenna is (played, playing) on their team.

9. Everyone is (talked, talking) about all the games they've won.

DIRECTIONS ▷ **Add ed or ing to each verb. Then, rewrite each sentence.**

10. Carmen help _____ Grandma cook yesterday.

_____

11. Grandma is cook _____ some soup today.

_____

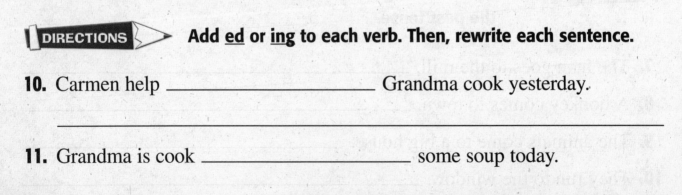

Using <u>Is</u> or <u>Are</u>

Use <u>is</u> and <u>are</u> to tell about something that is happening now.
Use <u>is</u> to tell about one person, place, or thing. Use <u>are</u> to tell about
more than one person, place, or thing. Use <u>are</u> with the word <u>you</u>.
Examples:
> Judy <u>is</u> going.
> Lynne and Ed <u>are</u> skating.
> The cats <u>are</u> sleeping.
> You <u>are</u> lost. <u>Are</u> you scared?

DIRECTIONS Write <u>is</u> or <u>are</u> to complete each sentence correctly.

1. We _____ going to the park.

2. Al _____ going, too.

3. Kate and Mario _____ running.

4. She _____ the faster runner.

5. Where _____ the twins?

6. They _____ climbing a tree.

7. You _____ going to climb, too.

8. The children _____ having fun.

DIRECTIONS Write one sentence about a park using <u>is</u>. Then, write one sentence about a park using <u>are</u>.

9. (is) _____

10. (are) _____

Using Was or Were

Use <u>was</u> and <u>were</u> to tell about something that happened in the past.
Use <u>was</u> to tell about one person, place, or thing. Use <u>were</u> to tell about more than one person, place, or thing. Use <u>were</u> with the word <u>you</u>.
Examples:

My bat <u>was</u> on the step.
Ten people <u>were</u> there.
You <u>were</u> late. <u>Were</u> you home?

▌DIRECTIONS ▷   **Circle the correct verb in ( ) to complete each sentence.**

1. The children (was, were) indoors while it rained.

2. José (was, were) reading a book.

3. Scott and Jay (was, were) playing checkers.

4. Ann, Roy, and Jami (was, were) playing cards.

5. Sara and Tara (was, were) talking.

6. Nick (was, were) beating a drum.

7. I (was, were) drawing pictures.

8. You (was, were) dancing.

▌DIRECTIONS ▷   **Write one sentence about a rainy day using <u>was</u>. Then, write one sentence about a rainy day using <u>were</u>.**

9. (was) _____

10. (were) _____

Using See, Sees, or Saw

Use see or sees to tell what is happening now. Use see with the words you and I. Use saw to tell what happened in the past.
Examples:

One boy sees a dog. Two boys see a dog.

I see a dog. Do you see a dog?

Justin saw Natalie last week.

◎ ◎ ◎ ◎

DIRECTIONS > **Write see, sees, or saw to complete each sentence correctly.**

1. Today Mike _____ his friend Lori.

2. He _____ her last Monday.

3. Lori _____ Mike paint now.

4. My dad _____ Mike paint now, too.

5. Mike _____ a beautiful sky last night.

6. He _____ pink in the sky on Sunday.

7. Grandpa and I _____ some trains now.

8. We _____ many trains on my last birthday.

9. We _____ old and new trains last winter.

10. Today I can _____ the train show.

DIRECTIONS > **Write see, sees, or saw. Then, rewrite each sentence.**

11. Last week we _____ Lee.

_____

12. Lee _____ my painting now.

_____

Using <u>Run</u>, <u>Runs</u>, or <u>Ran</u>

Use <u>run</u> or <u>runs</u> to tell what is happening now. Use <u>run</u> with the words <u>you</u> and <u>I</u>. Use <u>ran</u> to tell what happened in the past.
Examples:

One horse <u>runs</u>. Two horses <u>run</u>.
I <u>run</u> in the park. Do you <u>run</u>?
Yesterday we <u>ran</u> to the park.

DIRECTIONS ▷ **Write <u>run</u>, <u>runs</u>, or <u>ran</u>. Then, rewrite each sentence.**

1. Horses _____ wild long ago.

_____

2. A horse can _____ ten miles every day.

_____

3. Can you _____ as fast as a horse?

_____

4. Mandy _____ in a race last week.

_____

5. Carl _____ home from school now.

_____

6. Now Mandy _____ after Carl.

_____

7. How far can you _____?

_____

Using <u>Give</u>, <u>Gives</u>, or <u>Gave</u>

Use <u>give</u> or <u>gives</u> to tell what is happening now. Use <u>give</u> with the words <u>you</u> and <u>I</u>. Use <u>gave</u> to tell what happened in the past.
Examples:
    One student <u>gives</u> a gift. Two students <u>give</u> a gift.
    I <u>give</u> a gift. Do you <u>give</u> one?
    Jenna <u>gave</u> me a present yesterday.

 **Read the sentences. Circle the correct verb in ( ) to complete each sentence.**

1. Can you (give, gives, gave) the animals some food?

2. Sandi (give, gives, gave) them water yesterday.

3. Juan (give, gives, gave) the chickens corn now.

4. Chickens (give, gives, gave) us eggs to eat yesterday.

5. We (give, gives, gave) the kittens some milk last night.

6. Who (give, gives, gave) hay to the cow then?

7. Our cow (give, gives, gave) us milk yesterday.

8. I (give, gives, gave) food to the pigs last Monday.

 **Write three sentences about gifts using <u>give</u>, <u>gives</u>, and <u>gave</u>.**

9. (give) _____

10. (gives) _____

11. (gave) _____

Using **D**o or **D**oes

Use <u>does</u> to tell about one person, place, or thing.
Use <u>do</u> to tell about more than one person, place, or thing. Also use <u>do</u> with the words <u>you</u> and <u>I</u>.
Examples:
William <u>does</u> the work.
They <u>do</u> the work.
I <u>do</u> the work. You <u>do</u> the work.

DIRECTIONS > Write <u>do</u> or <u>does</u> to complete each sentence correctly.

1. We _____ a lot of work in the house.

2. My dad _____ all the dishes.

3. My mom _____ the windows.

4. My sister _____ the sweeping.

5. My grandma _____ the sewing.

6. I _____ the floor.

7. My little brother _____ the dusting.

8. I _____ not cook dinner.

9. My little sister _____ put away toys.

10. We all _____ some work in our house.

DIRECTIONS > Write one sentence about yourself using <u>do</u>. Then, write one sentence about a friend using <u>does</u>.

11. _____

12. _____

Using <u>Has</u>, <u>Have</u>, or <u>Had</u>

Use <u>has</u> to tell about one person, place, or thing. Use <u>have</u> to tell about more than one person, place, or thing. Use <u>have</u> with the words <u>you</u> and <u>I</u>. Use <u>had</u> to tell about the past.
Examples:

Jesse <u>has</u> a bird.
Cars <u>have</u> tires.
You <u>have</u> new shoes. I <u>have</u> fun.
My dogs <u>had</u> fleas. Bill <u>had</u> a cat last year.

DIRECTIONS   **Circle the correct verb in ( ) to complete each sentence.**

1. My brother (has, have, had) a pet fish last year.

2. Now Dan (has, have, had) a pet mouse.

3. The pets (has, have, had) good homes now.

4. I (has, have, had) a football now.

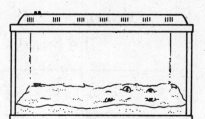

5. Now Dana (has, have, had) a pair of roller skates, too.

6. Yesterday Dawn (has, have, had) a full balloon.

7. Now the balloon (has, have, had) a hole in it.

8. She (has, have, had) the money to buy another balloon today.

DIRECTIONS   **Write <u>has</u>, <u>have</u>, or <u>had</u> to complete each sentence correctly.**

9. You _____ many friends now.

10. Your friends _____ fun together last Saturday.

11. Last week I _____ supper with Eric.

12. Now he _____ supper with me.

Adjectives

An **adjective** is a describing word. A describing word describes a noun.

Example:

The <u>old</u> woman walked home.

Describing words can tell about color or size.

Example:

<u>Red</u> flowers grow in the <u>small</u> garden.

Describing words can tell about shape.

Example:

The house has a <u>square</u> window.

Describing words can tell how something feels, tastes, sounds, or smells.

Example:

The flowers have a <u>sweet</u> smell.

DIRECTIONS Finish the sentences. Add describing words from the box.

| round | long | brown | tiny | pink | juicy | **WORD BOX** |

1. The woman puts on a _____ bonnet.

2. She walks down a _____ road.

3. Some _____ squirrels run by.

4. A man gives her a _____ orange.

5. The orange is _____.

6. Do you see a _____ bone in the yard?

Adjectives, page 2

Adjectives are describing words. Describing words can describe feelings.

Examples:

The woman was <u>surprised</u>.

She was <u>happy</u>.

Describing words can also tell how many.

Example:

She picked <u>four</u> flowers.

Some describing words that tell how many do not tell exact numbers.

Examples:

There are <u>many</u> roses in the garden.

<u>Some</u> grass grows here.

DIRECTIONS ▷ **Finish the sentences. Add describing words from the box.**

| happy | some | hungry | tired | three | sleepy | one | many | **WORD BOX** |

1. The woman was _____ from walking so far.

2. She was _____ to be home.

3. First, she put _____ flowers in a vase.

4. Next, she put _____ bone in a pot.

5. She was _____ and wanted to eat.

6. Then, she ate _____ soup.

7. She also had _____ crackers.

8. Last, the woman was _____ and went to bed.

Adjectives That Compare

Add <u>er</u> to most describing words when they are used to compare two things.
Example:
> This tree is <u>taller</u> than that one.

Add <u>est</u> to most describing words when they are used to compare more than two things.
Example:
> The sequoia tree is the <u>tallest</u> tree of all.

 **DIRECTIONS** → **Read the chart. Fill in the missing describing words.**

1.	long	longer	longest
2.	bright		brightest
3.	tall	taller	
4.		faster	fastest

DIRECTIONS → **Circle the correct describing word in ( ) to complete each sentence.**

5. That tree trunk is (thick, thicker) than this one.

6. The giant sequoia is the (bigger, biggest) living thing of all.

7. The stump of a giant sequoia is (wider, widest) than my room.

8. These trees are the (older, oldest) of all.

Using A or An

A and an are called articles. They are special adjectives.
Use an before words that begin with a vowel sound. The vowels
are a, e, i, o, and u.
Use a before words that begin with a consonant sound.
Examples:

an apple, an egg
a car, a skate

DIRECTIONS Choose the correct article. Write **a** or **an** before each word.

1. _____ arm
2. _____ dog
3. _____ hat
4. _____ ant
5. _____ cat
6. _____ elf

7. _____ ear
8. _____ office
9. _____ fire
10. _____ cow
11. _____ uncle
12. _____ tree

13. _____ inch
14. _____ ax
15. _____ top
16. _____ boat
17. _____ duck
18. _____ eagle

DIRECTIONS Write **a** or **an** to complete each sentence correctly.

19. Randy put _____ apple in my box.

20. Victor has _____ old bike.

21. Linda has two balls and _____ bat.

22. I have _____ sweet apple.

Sentences

A **sentence** is a group of words that tells or asks something. It gives a complete thought. Every sentence begins with a capital letter. Every sentence ends with a punctuation mark.
Examples:

    Friends play.

    Cars go fast.

> **DIRECTIONS**   **Write <u>yes</u> if the group of words is a sentence. Write <u>no</u> if the group of words is not a sentence.**

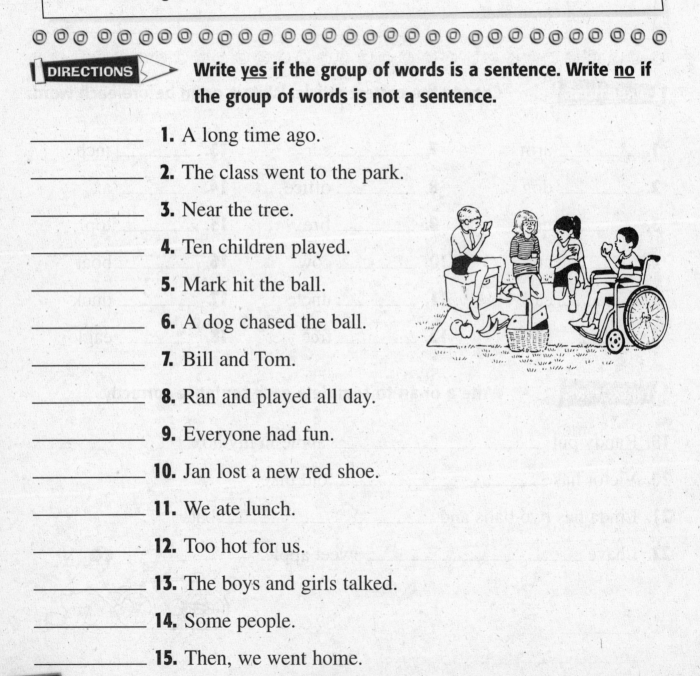

_____ 1. A long time ago.

_____ 2. The class went to the park.

_____ 3. Near the tree.

_____ 4. Ten children played.

_____ 5. Mark hit the ball.

_____ 6. A dog chased the ball.

_____ 7. Bill and Tom.

_____ 8. Ran and played all day.

_____ 9. Everyone had fun.

_____ 10. Jan lost a new red shoe.

_____ 11. We ate lunch.

_____ 12. Too hot for us.

_____ 13. The boys and girls talked.

_____ 14. Some people.

_____ 15. Then, we went home.

Sentences, page 2

Remember that a sentence tells a complete thought.
Examples:
    Mari caught the ball.
    Chad read a book.

DIRECTIONS ▷ **Draw lines between the groups of words to make sentences. Then, read the sentences.**

1.	Mrs. Brown	live in our building.
2.	Our building	is made of wood.
3.	Four families	lives on my street.
4.	Our class	was climbing the tree.
5.	Jennifer	went on a picnic.
6.	The sun	shone all day.
7.	Corn and beans	fed the baby goat.
8.	The wagon	has a broken wheel.
9.	The mother goat	grow on a farm.
10.	The boat	sailed in strong winds.
11.	The fisher	were sold in the store.
12.	Some of the fish	caught seven fish.
13.	Our team	hit the ball a lot.
14.	Our batters	won ten games.
15.	The ballpark	was full of fans.

DIRECTIONS ▷ **Write a sentence about your birthday.**

16. _____

_____

Sentence Parts

Every sentence has two parts. The **naming part** tells who or what the sentence is about. The naming part is called the subject.
The **action part** tells something about the naming part. The action part is called the predicate.
A naming part and an action part make a complete thought.
Examples:

Naming Part	Action Part
Sara	plants some seeds.

DIRECTIONS ▷ **Each group of words needs a naming part or an action part. Add words to make each group of words a complete sentence.**

1. John _____ .

2. Sara _____ .

3. _____ need sunshine and rain.

4. The flower seeds _____ .

5. John and Sara _____ .

6. _____ looks at the flower.

7. _____ grow in the garden.

8. The flowers _____ .

9. _____ bloom in the spring.

10. _____ are my favorite flowers.

11. The butterflies _____ .

12. _____ makes the flowers grow.

Naming Part of Sentences

> The naming part of a sentence tells who or what the sentence is about.
>
> *Examples:*
>
> <u>Three mice</u> run away.
> <u>The cat</u> plays with a ball.

◎ ◎

DIRECTIONS ▷ **Circle the naming part of each sentence.**

1. My family and I live on a busy street.

2. Sami Harper found a bird.

3. Miss Jenkins drives very slowly.

4. Mr. Chang walks his dog.

5. Henry throws to his dog.

6. Mr. Byrne cuts his grass.

7. Mrs. Lee picks up her children.

8. Mr. and Mrs. Diaz shop for food.

9. Jeanine plays in the park.

10. Mr. Wolf brings the mail.

11. Amy Taft brings the paper.

12. Mr. Dowd cooks dinner.

13. Mrs. Clark washes her windows.

14. Carolyn and Alberto plant flower seeds.

15. Julie waters the garden.

Action Part of Sentences

The action part of a sentence tells what someone or something does.
Examples:

Three mice <u>run away</u>.

The cat <u>plays with a ball</u>.

○○○ ○○ ○○○○○○ ○○ ○ ○○○ ○○○ ○ ○○○ ○○ ○○○○○ ○○○ ○ ○○ ○

DIRECTIONS ▷ **Choose an action part from the box to complete each sentence. Write it on the line.**

| barks | buzz | fly | hops | moo | cluck | quack | roar | **WORD BOX** |

1. Robins and blackbirds _____.

2. Yellow bees _____.

3. My little dog _____.

4. Mother Duck and her babies _____.

5. A rabbit with big feet _____.

6. Angry lions _____.

7. All the cows on the farm _____.

8. Chickens _____.

DIRECTIONS ▷ **Write a sentence about an animal that you like. Circle the naming part. Underline the action part.**

_____

_____

Word Order in Sentences

Words in a sentence must be in an order that makes sense.
Examples:
Grandpa plays baseball.
My sister writes stories.

DIRECTIONS ▸ **Write each group of words in an order that makes sense. Be sure to put a period at the end of each sentence.**

1. brother My apples eats

_____

2. drinks Elizabeth milk

_____

3. butter peanut Kim likes

_____

4. Justin bread wants

_____

5. corn plants Chris

_____

6. a fish Chang caught

_____

7. breakfast cooks Dad

_____

8. his shares Shawn lunch

_____

9. the Rosa grew carrot

_____

Telling Sentences and Asking Sentences

A **telling sentence** is a group of words that tells something. A telling sentence is also called a statement.

Examples:

I fed my pony.

Ponies like to run and play.

An **asking sentence** is a group of words that asks a question. You can answer an asking sentence. An asking sentence is also called a question.

Examples:

How old are you?

Where do you live?

◎ ◎

DIRECTIONS Write <u>telling</u> on the line before the group of words if it is a telling sentence. Write <u>asking</u> on the line before the group of words if it is an asking sentence. Leave the line blank if the group of words is not a sentence.

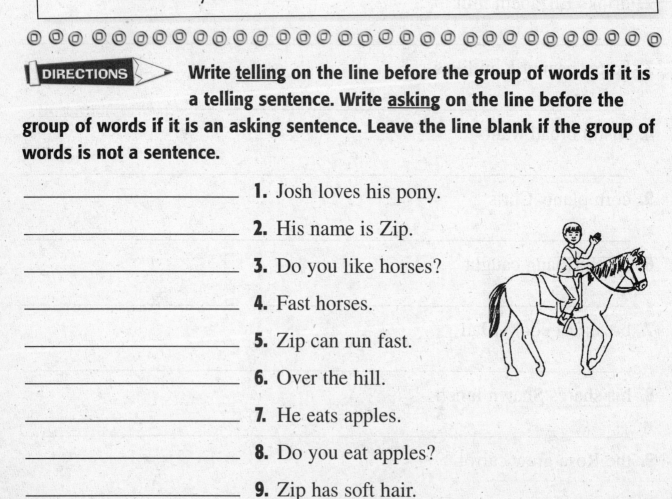

_____ **1.** Josh loves his pony.

_____ **2.** His name is Zip.

_____ **3.** Do you like horses?

_____ **4.** Fast horses.

_____ **5.** Zip can run fast.

_____ **6.** Over the hill.

_____ **7.** He eats apples.

_____ **8.** Do you eat apples?

_____ **9.** Zip has soft hair.

Kinds of Sentences

A **statement** is a sentence that tells something. It begins with a capital letter. It ends with a period **(.)**.
Example:
> John gives some seeds to Sara.

A **question** is a sentence that asks something. It begins with a capital letter. It ends with a question mark **(?)**.
Example:
> Will Sara plant seeds?

An **exclamation** is a sentence that shows strong feeling. It begins with a capital letter. It ends with an exclamation point **(!)**.
Example:
> What a fine garden John has!

DIRECTIONS Read the sentences. Write <u>statement</u> for a telling sentence. Write <u>question</u> for an asking sentence. Write <u>exclamation</u> for a sentence that shows strong feeling.

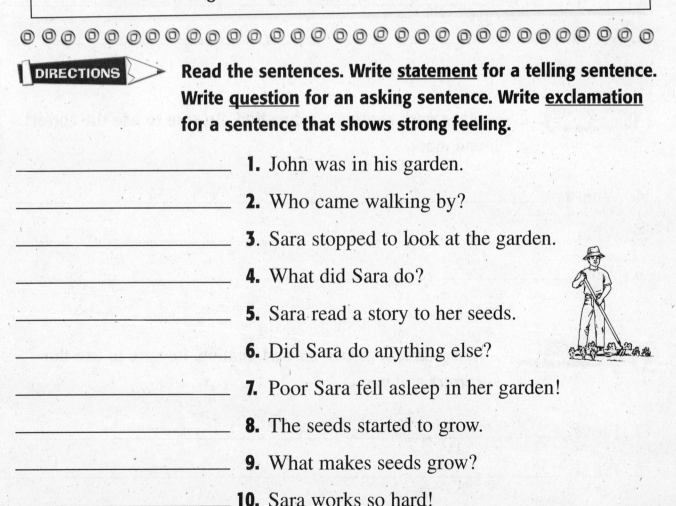

_____ **1.** John was in his garden.

_____ **2.** Who came walking by?

_____ **3.** Sara stopped to look at the garden.

_____ **4.** What did Sara do?

_____ **5.** Sara read a story to her seeds.

_____ **6.** Did Sara do anything else?

_____ **7.** Poor Sara fell asleep in her garden!

_____ **8.** The seeds started to grow.

_____ **9.** What makes seeds grow?

_____ **10.** Sara works so hard!

Kinds of Sentences, page 2

Use a statement to tell something. End a statement with a period.
Use a question to ask something. End a question with a question mark.
Use an exclamation to show strong feeling. End an exclamation with an exclamation point.

DIRECTIONS ▷ **Make each sentence a statement. Be sure to use the correct end mark.**

1. My favorite animal is _____

2. My favorite food is _____

3. My favorite color is _____

DIRECTIONS ▷ **Make each sentence a question. Be sure to use the correct end mark.**

4. What is _____

5. Where _____

6. Why _____

DIRECTIONS ▷ **Make each sentence an exclamation. Be sure to use the correct end mark.**

7. I love _____

8. It's so _____

Joining Sentences

A good writer can join two short sentences. This makes the sentences more interesting to read. The word <u>and</u> is used to join the sentences.

Sometimes the naming parts of two sentences are the same. The action parts can be joined.

Example:

John planted seeds. John worked in his garden.
John planted seeds <u>and</u> worked in his garden.

How to Join Sentences
1. Look for sentences that have the same naming part.
2. Write the naming part.
3. Look for different action parts. Use the word <u>and</u> to join them.
4. Write the new sentence.

 **Use the word <u>and</u> to join each pair of sentences. Write the new sentences.**

1. John gave seeds to Sara. John told her to plant them.

_____

2. Sara planted the seeds. Sara looked at the ground.

_____

3. Sara sang songs to her seeds. Sara read stories to them.

_____

4. The rain fell on the seeds. The rain helped them grow.

_____

Joining Sentences, page 2

A good writer can join two short sentences. This makes the sentences more interesting to read. The word <u>and</u> is used to join the sentences.

Sometimes the action parts of two sentences are the same. Then, the naming parts can be joined.

Example:

> The hunter stopped at the house. The bear stopped at the house.
> The hunter <u>and</u> the bear stopped at the house.

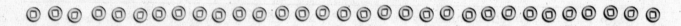

How to Join Sentences

1. Look for sentences that have the same action part.
2. Join the naming parts. Use the word <u>and</u>.
3. Add the action part.

 Use the word <u>and</u> to join each pair of sentences. Write the new sentences.

1. The farmer stood in the doorway. His family stood in the doorway.

_____

2. The hunter stayed with the family. The bear stayed with the family.

_____

3. The mice ran out the door. The children ran out the door.

_____

4. The hunter went home. The bear went home.

_____

Adding Describing Words to Sentences

A good writer adds describing words to sentences to give a clear picture.
Example:

The moth sat on top of a clover.
The <u>black</u> moth sat on top of a <u>white</u> clover.

How to Add Describing Words to Sentences
1. Look for sentences that do not give your reader a clear picture.
2. Think of describing words that tell more about what things look like.
3. Add the describing words to the sentences.

 **Add describing words to these sentences. Write the new sentences.**

1. The clown wears a hat.

_____

2. A lion jumps through a hoop.

_____

3. A monkey rides on an elephant.

_____

4. A butterfly flew into the tent.

_____

Beginning Sentences in Different Ways

A good writer should not begin every sentence with the same noun. Sometimes the words <u>he</u>, <u>she</u>, <u>I</u>, <u>we</u>, and <u>they</u> are used in place of nouns.

Example:

Ant climbed down a branch. Ant was thirsty. <u>She</u> tried to get a drink.

How to Begin Sentences in Different Ways

1. Look for sentences that begin with the same noun.
2. Use the word <u>he</u>, <u>she</u>, <u>I</u>, <u>we</u>, or <u>they</u> in place of the noun.
3. Write the new sentence.

 **Change the way some of these sentences begin. Begin some of them with <u>He</u>, <u>She</u>, <u>I</u>, <u>We</u>, or <u>They</u>. Write the new sentences.**

1. The ant climbed down a blade of grass. The ant fell into the spring.

_____

2. The bird pulled off a leaf. The bird let the leaf fall into the water.

_____

3. The hunter saw a lion. The hunter spread his net.

_____

4. The lion and I live in the woods. The lion and I are friends.

_____

Writing Clear Sentences

A good writer uses exact verbs. These are verbs that give a clear picture of an action.

Example:

       Spaceships <u>go</u> to the Moon.
       Spaceships <u>zoom</u> to the Moon.

How to Use Exact Verbs in Sentences

1. Picture the action. Think about what a person or thing is doing.
2. Choose an action verb that tells exactly what the person or thing is doing.
3. Use the action verb in a sentence.

 **Think of a more exact verb for each underlined verb. Write the new word on the line.**

1. People <u>walk</u> to work. _____

2. Trains <u>move</u> along the tracks. _____

3. We <u>ride</u> our bicycles. _____

4. Fast cars <u>go</u> up the road. _____

5. The airplane <u>flies</u> in the sky. _____

6. A man <u>runs</u> around the park. _____

7. The children <u>walk</u> to school. _____

8. A bus <u>goes</u> down the highway. _____

9. The boat <u>moves</u> along the shore. _____

Writing Names of People

Each word of a person's name begins with a capital letter.
Examples:

Mary Ann Miller

Michael Jordan

Grandma Moses

DIRECTIONS Rewrite the names. Use capital letters where they are needed.

1. mark twain _____

2. beverly cleary _____

3. diane dillon _____

4. alicia acker _____

5. ezra jack keats _____

DIRECTIONS Circle the letters that should be capital letters.

6. Today mother called grandma.

7. We will see grandma and grandpa at the party.

8. Will uncle carlos and aunt kathy be there, too?

DIRECTIONS Rewrite the sentences. Use capital letters where they are needed.

9. mario martinez told me a story.

_____

10. ichiro and I played ball.

_____

Writing Initials

An **initial** stands for a person's name. It is a capital letter with a
period **(.)** after it.
Examples:

Steven Bell Mathis = Steven **B**. Mathis or **S. B.** Mathis or **S. B. M.**

DIRECTIONS ▷ Write the initials of each name.

1. Clara Delrio _____

2. Carrie Anne Collier _____

3. Marcus Brown _____

4. Michael Tond _____

5. Keiko Senda _____

6. Terri Lynn Turner _____

7. Isaiah Bradley _____

8. Cata Lil Walker _____

DIRECTIONS ▷ Rewrite the names. Use initials for the names that are
underlined.

9. Joan Walsh Anglund

_____

10. Lee Bennett Hopkins

_____

11. Arturo Martinez

_____

12. Patricia Ann Rosen

_____

DIRECTIONS ▷ Rewrite the sentences. Be sure to write the initials correctly.

13. The box was for m s mills.

_____

14. d e ellis sent it to her.

_____

15. t j lee brought the box to the house.

_____

Writing Titles of Respect

Begin a **title of respect** with a capital letter.
End <u>Mr.</u>, <u>Mrs.</u>, <u>Ms.</u>, and <u>Dr.</u> with a period. They are short forms, or abbreviations, of longer words.
Do not end <u>Miss</u> with a period.
Examples:
    Mr. George Selden
    Dr. Martin Luther King
    Miss Jane Pittman

DIRECTIONS ▷ **Rewrite the names correctly. Place periods and capital letters where they are needed.**

1. mrs ruth scott _____

2. mr kurt wiese _____

3. miss e garcia _____

4. dr seuss _____

5. ms carol baylor _____

6. mr and mrs h cox _____

7. miss k e jones _____

8. dr s tomas rios _____

DIRECTIONS ▷ **Rewrite the sentences correctly. Place periods and capital letters where they are needed.**

9. mrs h stone is here to see dr brooks.

_____

10. mr f green and ms miller are not here.

_____

Writing Names of Places

The names of cities, states, and countries begin with a capital letter.
The names of streets, parks, lakes, rivers, and schools begin with a capital letter.
The abbreviations of the words <u>street</u>, <u>road</u>, and <u>drive</u> in a place name begin with a capital letter and end with a period.

Examples:

Reno, Nevada
Canada
First Street
Central Park
Red River
Road = Rd.   Dove Rd.

 **Rewrite the sentences. Use capital letters where they are needed.**

1. James lives in dayton, ohio.

_____

2. His house is on market st.

_____

3. I think thomas park is in this town.

_____

4. We went to mathis lake for a picnic.

_____

5. Is parker school far away?

_____

Writing Names of Days and Months

The names of days of the week begin with a capital letter.
The names of the months begin with a capital letter.
Examples:

　　　Monday, Friday　　　April, October

The abbreviations of the days of the week begin with a capital letter. They end with a period.

The abbreviations of the months begin with a capital letter. They end with a period. The names of May, June, and July are not usually abbreviated.

Examples:

　　Sun., Mon., Tues., Wed., Thurs., Fri., Sat.
　　Jan., Feb., Mar., Apr., Aug., Sept., Oct., Nov., Dec.

DIRECTIONS ▷ **Write the name of a day or month to complete each sentence.**

1. The day after Sunday is _____.

2. The day before Saturday is _____.

3. Valentine's Day is in _____.

4. A month in the summer is _____.

5. Thanksgiving Day is in _____.

DIRECTIONS ▷ **Write the correct abbreviation for each day or month. Be sure to end the abbreviation with a period.**

6. Tuesday _____　　9. Saturday _____

7. Thursday _____　　10. January _____

8. December _____　　11. September _____

Writing Names of Holidays

Each important word in the name of a holiday begins with a capital letter.
Examples:
    Valentine's Day
    Memorial Day
    Fourth of July

DIRECTIONS ▷ **Write the holiday names correctly.**

1. new year's day _____

2. mother's day _____

3. independence day _____

4. labor day _____

5. cinco de mayo _____

6. thanksgiving day _____

7. veterans day _____

DIRECTIONS ▷ **Rewrite each sentence correctly.**

8. earth day is in April.

_____

9. boxing day is a British holiday.

_____

10. father's day is in June.

_____

Writing Titles of Books, Stories, and Poems

Begin the first word and last word in the title of a book with a capital letter. All other words begin with a capital letter except unimportant words. Some unimportant words are <u>a</u>, <u>an</u>, <u>the</u>, <u>of</u>, <u>with</u>, <u>for</u>, <u>at</u>, <u>in</u>, and <u>on</u>. Draw a line under the title of a book.
Examples:

<u>The Snowy Day</u>

<u>Storm at Sea</u>

Begin the first word, last word, and all important words in the title of a story or poem with a capital letter. Put quotation marks (" ") around the title of a story or poem.
Examples:

"Jonas and the Monster" (story)

"Something Is Out There" (poem)

 **Write these book titles correctly. Be sure to underline the title of a book.**

1. best friends

2. the biggest bear

3. rabbits on roller skates

4. down on the sunny farm

 **Read the sentences. Circle the letters that should be capital letters.**

5. My favorite poem is called "we bees."

6. I read a story called "the dancing pony" last week.

7. Robert Louis Stevenson wrote a poem called "my shadow."

8. Lori wrote a story named "my summer on the farm."

Beginning Sentences

Begin the first word of a sentence with a capital letter.
Examples:

The garden is very pretty.
Flowers grow there.
What kind of flowers do you see?

◎◎◎◎ ◎◎ ◎◎ ◎◎◎ ◎◎ ◎◎◎ ◎◎◎ ◎◎ ◎◎ ◎◎◎ ◎◎◎ ◎◎ ◎◎◎ ◎◎

DIRECTIONS ▷ **Rewrite these sentences. Begin each sentence with a capital letter.**

1. there are many kinds of gardens.

_____

2. vegetables grow in some gardens.

_____

3. you can find gardens in parks.

_____

4. i like to work in the garden.

_____

5. deb likes to play ball.

_____

6. her ball is red.

_____

7. jet wants to play.

_____

8. deb throws the ball.

_____

9. the ball goes far.

_____

Ending Sentences

Put a **period (.)** at the end of a sentence that tells something.
Examples:

Patty is my friend.
We play together.

Put a **question mark (?)** at the end of a sentence that asks something.
Examples:

Is he your brother?
Do you have a sister?

 **Rewrite these telling sentences. Use capital letters and periods where they are needed.**

1. patty played on the baseball team

_____

2. patty hit two home runs

_____

3. she caught the ball, too

_____

 **Rewrite these asking sentences. Use capital letters and question marks where they are needed.**

4. what time is it

_____

5. is it time for lunch

_____

6. are you ready to eat

_____

Periods

Use a **period (.)** at the end of a statement.
Example:
> I like to read books about frogs.

Put a period at the end of most titles of people.
Example:
> Mr. Arnold Lobel wrote the book.

These are titles of people.
> Mr.   Mrs.   Ms.   Dr.   Miss

DIRECTIONS Correct the sentences. Add periods where they are needed.

1. John has a nice garden

2. The flowers are pretty

3. John gave Sara some seeds

4. Sara will plant them in the ground

5. Little green plants will grow

6. Ms Sara thought the seeds were afraid.

7. Mr John told Sara not to worry.

8. Mrs Jones told Sara to wait a few days.

9. Sara showed her garden to Dr Dewey.

10. Ms Babbitt thinks Sara has a nice garden.

Question Marks, Exclamation Points, and Apostrophes

Use a **question mark (?)** at the end of a question.
Example:
Who are you?
Use an **exclamation point (!)** at the end of an exclamation.
Example:
Leave me alone!
Use an **apostrophe (')** to show that one or more letters have been left out in a contraction.
Example:
His parents didn't take Stewart anywhere.

 **DIRECTIONS** Finish the sentences correctly. Add question marks and exclamation points where they are needed.

1. Stewart just does not care

2. Would you rather stay here

3. Does Stewart care about anything

4. Yes, indeed he cares

 **DIRECTIONS** Circle the correct contraction in ( ) to complete each sentence.

5. Stewart said, "I (dont, don't) care!"

6. "(Ill, I'll) get you," said the bear.

7. Stewart (didn't, didnt) want to stay with the bear.

Using Apostrophes in Contractions

A **contraction** is a word made by joining two words. An **apostrophe (')** shows where a letter or letters are left out.
Examples:

    is not = isn't
    cannot = can't
    do not = don't
    are not = aren't

◎ ◎◎ ◎◎ ◎◎◎ ◎◎ ◎◎ ◎◎◎ ◎◎ ◎◎◎ ◎◎◎ ◎◎◎ ◎◎◎ ◎◎ ◎◎ ◎

DIRECTIONS ▷ **Draw a line from the two words to the contraction.**

1. were not   hasn't

2. was not   haven't

3. has not   wasn't

4. have not   weren't

5. did not   aren't

6. are not   didn't

DIRECTIONS ▷ **Write each contraction as two words.**

7. isn't _____ _____   **11.** didn't _____ _____

8. don't _____ _____   **12.** hadn't _____ _____

9. wasn't _____ _____   **13.** doesn't _____ _____

10. can't _____ _____   **14.** aren't _____ _____

DIRECTIONS ▷ **Write a contraction for the two words.**

15. Today (is not) _____ a good day.

16. I (do not) _____ have my lunch.

17. I (did not) _____ finish my work.

Commas

Use a **comma (,)** between the name of a city and a state.

Examples:

Toledo, Ohio

Albany, New York

Use a comma (,) between the day and the year in a date.

Examples:

July 4, 1776

November 1, 2003

Use a comma (,) after the greeting and after the closing in a letter.

Examples:

Dear Mom and Dad,

Your friend,

DIRECTIONS Read Mary Jane's letter to Grandmother. Put commas where they are needed.

June 8 2003

Dear Grandmother

    I hope you are feeling better. Yesterday Mom and I went shopping. We found a pretty new jacket for you. The tag says it comes from Chicago Illinois. I hope you like the jacket. Please write to me soon.

Love

Mary Jane

Using Commas in Place Names

Put a comma between the name of a city and its state. Names of cities and states begin with a capital letter.

Examples:

    Denver, Colorado

    Dover, Delaware

DIRECTIONS > **Write the names of the cities and states correctly. Put commas where they are needed.**

1. akron ohio   _____

2. hilo hawaii   _____

3. macon georgia   _____

4. nome alaska   _____

5. provo utah   _____

DIRECTIONS > **Rewrite the sentences. Use capital letters and commas where they are needed.**

6. Nancy lives in barnet vermont.

_____

7. Mr. Hill went to houston texas.

_____

8. Did Bruce like bend oregon?

_____

9. Will Amy visit newark ohio?

_____

10. How far away is salem maine?

_____

Using Commas in Dates

Put a comma between the day of the month and the year.
Examples:
    March 2, 1836
    January 1, 2003

DIRECTIONS ▷ **Write these dates correctly. Use capital letters, periods, and commas where they are needed.**

1. dec 12 1948 _____

2. mar 27 1965 _____

3. sept 8 1994 _____

4. nov 1 2000 _____

5. jan 5 1995 _____

DIRECTIONS ▷ **Complete the sentences. Write the date correctly on the line.**

6. Jim was born on _____. (august 10 1967)

7. Jen's birthday is _____. (Oct 17 1983)

8. Maria visited on _____. (february 8 1991)

9. Dad's party was on _____. (july 29 1989)

10. Carrie started school on _____. (sept 3 2001)

11. Luis lost his first tooth on _____. (oct 20 1998)

12. I was born on _____.

Rhyming Words

Words that end with the same sounds are **rhyming words**. Here are some rhyming words.

Examples: car—star   boat—goat

A **rhyme** is two or more lines that end with rhyming words. Many rhymes are silly or funny.

Examples: The cat took a rocket trip to the <u>moon</u>.
               It left in July and came back in <u>June</u>.

How to Write a Rhyme
1. Write two lines.
2. End each line with a rhyming word.

 **DIRECTIONS**   **Choose a word from the box to finish each rhyme.**

cow	dog	bee	hat	**WORD BOX**

1. Did you ever see a cat

   Wear a funny _____?

2. The cat climbed up a tree

   And sang a song with a _____.

3. The bee said, "Meow,"

   And flew away to visit the _____.

4. The cow watched a frog

   Hop over a _____.

Synonyms

Words that mean almost the same thing are called **synonyms**.
Examples:

Grin is a synonym of smile.

Sleep is a synonym of rest.

◎◎◎ ◎◎ ◎◎◎◎◎◎◎◎◎◎◎◎◎◎◎◎◎◎ ◎◎◎◎◎◎◎◎◎◎◎ ◎

> **DIRECTIONS** **Read each sentence. Find a synonym in the box for each underlined word. Write it on the line.**

						WORD BOX
dog	dad	gift	large	great	home	
road	sad	sick	sleep	small	yell	

1. I walked across the <u>street</u>. _____

2. I went into my <u>house</u>. _____

3. I was so <u>unhappy</u>. _____

4. I almost felt <u>ill</u>. _____

5. It was my birthday. No one gave me a <u>present</u>. _____

6. Then I saw something <u>little</u>. _____

7. It had <u>big</u> eyes. _____

8. It was a little <u>puppy</u>. _____

9. I began to <u>shout</u>. _____

10. "What a <u>wonderful</u> present!" _____

11. My <u>father</u> did remember my birthday. _____

12. I don't think I will <u>rest</u> tonight. _____

◎◎◎ ◎◎ ◎◎◎◎ ◎◎◎ ◎◎◎ ◎◎◎ ◎◎◎ ◎◎◎ ◎◎◎ ◎

Antonyms

Words that mean the opposite are called **antonyms**.
Examples:

Up is an antonym of down.

Day is an antonym of night.

◎ ◎◎ ◎◎ ◎◎◎ ◎◎◎ ◎◎◎ ◎◎◎ ◎◎◎ ◎◎◎ ◎◎ ◎◎◎ ◎◎◎ ◎◎ ◎◎◎

DIRECTIONS ➤ **Draw a line to the antonym for each underlined word.**

1. a <u>hard</u> bed   dark
2. a <u>short</u> story   happy
3. a <u>light</u> color   long
4. <u>off</u> the table   low
5. a <u>sad</u> movie   on
6. a <u>high</u> bridge   soft

DIRECTIONS ➤ **Write the antonym for the underlined word.**

7. When you are not <u>wet</u>, you are _____.
(happy, dry)

8. I like to run <u>fast</u>, not _____.
(slow, far)

9. When food isn't <u>good</u>, it tastes _____.
(hot, bad)

10. Summer is <u>hot</u>, and winter is _____.
(cold, snow)

11. A traffic light turns red for <u>stop</u> and green for _____.
(high, go)

12. Some questions are <u>easy</u>. Others are _____.
(not, hard)

Homographs

Homographs are words that are spelled alike but have different meanings. Some homographs are pronounced differently.
Example:

<u>felt</u>: a soft kind of cloth   <u>wind</u>: moving air
<u>felt</u>: sensed on the skin   <u>wind</u>: to turn a knob

◎◎◎ ◎◎ ◎◎◎◎ ◎◎◎ ◎◎◎ ◎◎◎ ◎◎◎ ◎◎◎ ◎◎◎ ◎◎◎ ◎◎◎ ◎◎◎ ◎◎◎ ◎◎◎ ◎◎◎ ◎◎◎ ◎◎

 **DIRECTIONS**   **Look at each pair of pictures. Read each sentence. Then, write the letter of the correct meaning on the line.**

bat

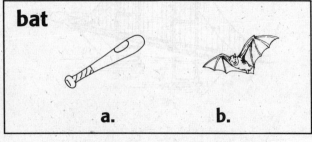

a.   b.

____ **1.** Tony has a wooden bat.

____ **2.** The bat sleeps during the day.

____ **3.** The bat broke when Alberto hit the ball.

pitcher

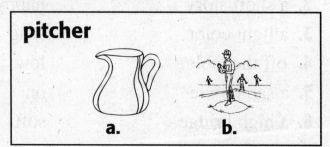

a.   b.

____ **7.** I put some juice in the pitcher.

____ **8.** The pitcher threw the ball too low.

____ **9.** The milk pitcher was empty.

plant

a.   b.

____ **4.** Kendra wants to plant a tree.

____ **5.** The farmer will plant his crops in the fall.

____ **6.** Jody grew a plant at school.

light

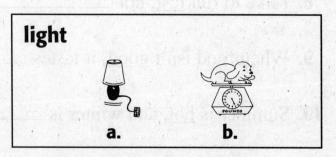

a.   b.

____ **10.** I will turn on the light.

____ **11.** The puppy is light.

____ **12.** There is only one light in my room.

◎◎◎ ◎◎◎ ◎◎◎ ◎◎ ◎◎◎ ◎◎◎ ◎◎◎ ◎◎ ◎◎ ◎◎◎ ◎◎ ◎◎◎ ◎◎ ◎◎◎ ◎◎◎ ◎◎

Homophones

Homophones are words that sound the same but are spelled differently.

Use <u>hear</u> to mean "to listen to."

Example:

    We <u>hear</u> the bell ringing.

Use <u>here</u> to mean "to this place" or "at this place."

Example:

    Bring the ticket <u>here</u>.

Use <u>your</u> when you mean "belonging to you."

Example:

    Do you have <u>your</u> homework?

Use <u>you're</u> when you mean "you are."

Example:

    <u>You're</u> in trouble now.

DIRECTIONS ▷ **Write <u>hear</u> or <u>here</u> to complete each sentence correctly.**

1. Did you _____ that the circus is coming?

2. Is it coming _____ soon?

3. Yes, it will be _____ today.

4. I think I _____ the music now.

DIRECTIONS ▷ **Write <u>your</u> or <u>you're</u> to complete each sentence correctly.**

5. _____ a good skater, Eric.

6. Pull _____ laces tight.

7. Now _____ ready to skate safely.

8. Were _____ legs this wobbly when you started?

More Homophones

Homophones are words that sound the same but are spelled differently.

Use <u>write</u> to mean "to put words on paper."

Example:

Please <u>write</u> your name on your paper.

Use <u>right</u> to mean "correct."

Example:

Your answer is <u>right</u>.

Use <u>right</u> to mean "the opposite of left."

Example:

Turn <u>right</u> to get to my school

DIRECTIONS ▷ **Write <u>right</u> or <u>write</u> to complete each sentence correctly.**

1. Chris likes to _____ on the board.

2. Everything was _____ on Martha's math paper.

3. We turn _____ to go to the lunchroom.

4. Our class is learning to _____ stories.

5. Kim drew the picture on the _____ side.

6. Luis can _____ in Spanish.

7. The teacher marked the _____ answers.

8. Be sure you do the _____ page.

9. Jenna will _____ about her birthday party.

10. James colors with his _____ hand.

Troublesome Words

Use <u>two</u> to mean "the number 2."
Example:
> <u>Two</u> children worked together.

Use <u>too</u> to mean "more than enough."
Example:
> There are <u>too</u> many people on the bus.

Use <u>too</u> to mean "also."
Example:
> May I help, <u>too</u>?

Use <u>to</u> to mean "toward" or "to do something."
Example:
> Let's go <u>to</u> the library <u>to</u> find Kim.

DIRECTIONS → **Write <u>two</u>, <u>too</u>, or <u>to</u> to complete each sentence.**

1. The children were working _____ make a class library.

2. Andy had _____ books in his hand.

3. He gave them _____ Ms. Diaz.

4. Ms. Diaz was happy _____ get the books.

5. "We can never have _____ many books," she said.

6. Rosa said she would bring _____ or three books.

7. James wanted to bring some, _____.

8. Joann found a book that was _____ old.

9. Pages started _____ fall out when she picked it up.

10. Soon everyone would have new books _____ read.

11. We can take out _____ of these books at a time.

More Troublesome Words

Use <u>there</u> when you mean "in that place."
Example:
   The dinosaur is over <u>there</u>.
Use <u>their</u> when you mean "belonging to them."
Example:
   This is <u>their</u> swamp.
<u>They're</u> is a contraction for <u>they are</u>. Use <u>they're</u> when you mean
"they are."
Example:
   <u>They're</u> eating leaves from the trees.

DIRECTIONS ▷ **Circle the correct word in ( ) to complete each sentence.**

1. Is this (their, they're) food?

2. (There, They're) huge animals.

3. A big one is over (there, their).

4. Once it was (there, their) land.

5. Dinosaurs lived (they're, there) for a while.

6. (They're, There) everywhere!

7. (They're, There) the two biggest dinosaurs.

8. The faster dinosaur is resting (their, there).

9. Small dinosaurs lived (they're, there) long ago.

10. (Their, There) land was different then.

11. I see some more dinosaurs over (they're, there).

12. (They're, There) in the lake.

Compound Words

Sometimes two words can be put together to make a new word.
The new word is called a **compound word**.
Examples:

>   lunch + room = lunchroom
>   every + day = everyday

 Write compound words. Pick words from Box 1 and Box 2.
Write the new word in Box 3.

Box 1	Box 2	Box 3
1. sun	noon	_____
2. after	glasses	_____
3. play	side	_____
4. birth	ground	_____
5. out	book	_____
6. scrap	day	_____

DIRECTIONS ▶ Write a compound word to finish each sentence. You may
use the compound words you made above.

7. Dana was wearing _____ in class.

8. In the _____, Dana was sent to the principal's office.

9. Brad put a picture of the school in his _____.

10. Brad will be eight years old on his next _____.

11. We can't go _____ if it rains.

12. The _____ will be too wet.

Prefixes

A **prefix** is a group of letters added to the beginning of a word.
Adding a prefix to a word changes its meaning.
Examples:

   The old woman was <u>happy</u>.
   The old woman was <u>unhappy</u>.

Prefix	Meaning	Example
un	not	<u>un</u>clear
re	again	<u>re</u>write

DIRECTIONS ▷ **Read each sentence. Underline the word that has a prefix. Tell the meaning of the word.**

1. The old man was unable to find something to wear.

_____

2. The old woman reopened the drawer.

_____

3. She told the old man they were unlucky.

_____

4. The old man felt this was unfair.

_____

5. He was very unhappy.

_____

6. The woman asked the man to rewind the yarn.

_____

7. The old woman rewashed the socks.

_____

8. Could the socks be uneven?

_____

9. The old man refilled his wife's glass.

_____

10. The farmer's wife reknitted the sweater.

_____

Suffixes

A **suffix** is a group of letters added to the end of a word. Adding a suffix to a word changes its meaning.

Examples:

Josef's parents were <u>helpless</u>.
The doctor was <u>helpful</u>.

Suffix	Meaning	Example
ful	full of	hope<u>ful</u>
less	without	use<u>less</u>
able	able to be	break<u>able</u>

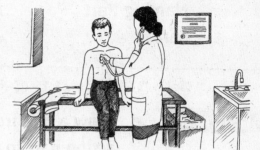

 **Read each sentence. Underline the word that has a suffix. Tell the meaning of the word.**

1. Is Josef careful? _____

2. Josef thought the game was harmless. _____

3. The chair Josef was on was breakable. _____

DIRECTIONS **Complete each sentence with a word from the box. Tell the meaning of the word you chose.**

hopeful	dreadful	thankful	**WORD BOX**

4. Josef's parents had a _____ shock!

_____

5. They were _____ the chair would not break.

_____

6. When Josef came out of the hospital, he was very _____.

_____

Writing Sentences

Remember that sentences have a naming part and an action part.
Example:

Naming Part	Action Part
Sara	won the race.

 **DIRECTIONS** ▷ **Draw a line from a naming part to an action part to make sentences.**

Naming Part	Action Part
1. Grandma	baked.
2. Aunt Sue	sings.
3. My friend	skates.
4. Earl's dad	reads.
5. Kiko's mom	cooks.
6. Jon's sister	played.

 **DIRECTIONS** ▷ **Write sentences with the naming parts and action parts you put together. Add some words of your own.**

7. _____

8. _____

9. _____

10. _____

11. _____

12. _____

Paragraphs

A **paragraph** is a group of sentences that tells about one main idea. The first line of a paragraph is indented. This means the first word is moved in a little from the left margin.

The first sentence in a paragraph often tells the main idea. The other sentences tell about the main idea.

Example:

A safe home keeps people from getting hurt. Shoes or toys should not be left on the stairs. Matches, medicines, and cleaners should be locked safely away. Grown-ups should get things that are on high shelves for children. Then, children will not fall and get hurt.

How to Write a Paragraph

1. Write a sentence that tells the main idea.
2. Indent the first line.
3. Write sentences that tell more about the main idea.

DIRECTIONS ▷ **Write three sentences that tell about this main idea.**

There are many things you can do to be safe at school.

_____

_____

_____

_____

_____

_____

Main Idea

The **main idea** of a paragraph is often in the first sentence. It tells what the paragraph is about.
Example:

> **I have nice neighbors.** Ms. Hill gives me flowers. Mr. Stone always smiles and waves. Miss Higgins plays ball with me.

⊚⊚⊚ ⊚⊚ ⊚⊚⊚⊚⊚⊚⊚ ⊚ ⊚⊚⊚ ⊚⊚⊚⊚⊚⊚ ⊚ ⊚⊚⊚⊚⊚⊚⊚ ⊚⊚ ⊚

▌DIRECTIONS ⟩ **Read each paragraph. Write the sentence that tells the main idea.**

Uncle Joe is a funny man. He tells jokes about elephants. He does magic tricks that don't work. He makes funny faces when he tells stories. He always makes me laugh.

1. _____

_____

Dad told us a funny story about his dog. When Dad was a little boy, he had a dog named Tiger. One day, Dad forgot his lunch. Dad said Tiger would bring it to school. A friend thought it would be a real tiger.

2. _____

_____

Firefighters are brave people. They go into burning buildings. They put out fires. They teach families how to be safe in their homes.

3. _____

_____

⊚⊚⊚ ⊚⊚⊚⊚⊚⊚ ⊚ ⊚ ⊚⊚⊚⊚⊚⊚ ⊚⊚ ⊚⊚⊚⊚⊚⊚⊚ ⊚⊚ ⊚

Supporting Details

The other sentences in a paragraph give **details** about the main idea in the beginning sentence.
Example:

I have nice neighbors. **Ms. Hill gives me flowers. Mr. Stone always smiles and waves. Miss Higgins plays ball with me.**

 **DIRECTIONS** Read each paragraph. Circle the main idea. Underline the sentences that give details about the main idea.

1. Uncle Joe is a funny man. He tells jokes about elephants. He does magic tricks that don't work. He makes funny faces when he tells stories. He always makes me laugh.

2. Dad told us a funny story about his dog. When Dad was a little boy, he had a dog named Tiger. One day Dad forgot his lunch. Dad said Tiger would bring it to school. A friend thought it would be a real tiger.

3. Firefighters are brave people. They go into burning buildings. They put out fires. They teach families how to be safe in their homes.

Order in Paragraphs

The sentences in a paragraph tell things in the order in which they happened.

Words such as <u>first</u>, <u>second</u>, <u>third</u>, <u>next</u>, <u>then</u>, and <u>last</u> can help tell when things happened.

Example:

Jane got ready for bed. **First**, she took a bath. **Next**, she brushed her teeth. **Then**, she put on her pajamas. **Last**, she read a story and got into bed.

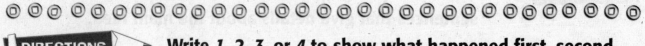

DIRECTIONS ➤ **Write *1*, *2*, *3*, or *4* to show what happened first, second, third, and last.**

Eva planted flowers. First, she got a shovel. Next, she dug some holes in the garden. Then, she put the flowers into the holes. Last, she put the shovel back in its place.

_____ Then, she put the flowers into the holes.

_____ Next, she dug some holes in the garden.

_____ Last, she put the shovel back in its place.

_____ First, she got a shovel.

Dan and Larry washed the car. First, they got the car wet. Next, they put soap all over it. Then, they washed all the soap off. Last, they dried the car.

_____ They put soap all over the car.

_____ They washed all the soap off.

_____ Dan and Larry dried the car.

_____ The boys got the car wet.

Personal Narrative

A **personal narrative** is a story about the writer. In a story, a writer tells about one main idea. Every story has a beginning, a middle, and an ending.

Example:

One day my grandfather and I went to the zoo. First, we looked at lions and tigers. Next, we watched the monkeys play. Then, we went to see the bears. Last, Grandfather helped me feed the seals. My day with Grandfather was wonderful!

How to Write a Paragraph About Yourself

1. Write a sentence that tells about something that happened to you. Tell where the story took place.
2. Write sentences that tell about what happened in order. Use the words <u>first</u>, <u>next</u>, <u>then</u>, and <u>last</u>.
3. Tell how the story ended.
4. Use the words <u>I</u> and <u>me</u>.
5. Give the story a title.

 **DIRECTIONS** **Read the *Example* paragraph above. Answer the questions.**

1. Where does the story take place?

_____

2. What happens after they look at the lions and tigers?

_____

3. What happens last?

_____

Personal Narrative, page 2

> **DIRECTIONS** **Finish the paragraph. Add words that tell about yourself.**

I had a good day at school. First, I _____

_____. Next, I _____

_____. Then, I ate lunch with my friend

_____.

Last, I _____

_____.

> **DIRECTIONS** **Finish the chart. Use the chart to write a story about yourself.**

Beginning	Middle	Ending
Who is in the story? Where does the story happen?	What happens?	How do things work out?

_____

_____

_____

_____

_____

_____

_____

Poem

In a **poem**, a writer paints a picture with words. Many poems have rhyming words at the end of every line or every other line.
Example:

Special Things

I like
White snow and blue bows.
I like
The sweet red rose.
I like
The crunchy sand between my toes.
I like
My puppy's wet, black nose.

How to Write a Poem
1. End some lines with rhyming words.
2. Try to paint a picture with words.
3. Give your poem a title.

 **Read the *Example* poem above. Answer the questions.**

1. What is the poem about?

_____

2. Name two rhyming words in the poem.

_____

3. Name two words that describe in the poem.

_____

Poem, page 2

DIRECTIONS Finish this poem. Think of describing words and words that rhyme. Give your poem a title.

_____

Summer is fun.

I can _____.

I feel so free

Like a _____.

DIRECTIONS Finish the chart. Use the chart to write a poem.

My title
_____

Describing words I will use	Rhyming words I will use
_____	_____
_____	_____
_____	_____

_____

_____

_____

_____

_____

Describing Paragraph

In a paragraph that **describes**, a writer tells about a person, place, or thing. The sentences have describing words that help the reader see, hear, taste, smell, and feel.

Example:

Many birds visit my backyard. Red cardinals make nests in our bushes. Many tiny hummingbirds buzz around the yellow flowers in our garden. Robins chirp sweetly and wake me in the morning.

How to Write a Paragraph That Describes

1. Write a sentence that tells whom or what the paragraph is about.
2. Write sentences that tell more about the main idea.
3. Use describing words in your sentences.

 **DIRECTIONS** Read the *Example* describing paragraph. Answer the questions.

1. What is the topic of the paragraph?

_____

2. Which words tell what the birds are like?

_____

3. Write a describing sentence to add to the paragraph.

_____

Describing Paragraph, page 2

Finish the paragraph. Add describing words.

The little woman put on her _____ hat.

She went outside. It was a _____ day. The sky was

_____. The little woman felt _____.

Finish the chart. Write describing words about your topic. Use the chart to write a describing paragraph.

My topic: _____

Looks	Feels	Tastes	Smells	Sounds
_____	_____	_____	_____	_____
_____	_____	_____	_____	_____
_____	_____	_____	_____	_____
_____	_____	_____	_____	_____

_____

_____

_____

_____

_____

_____

_____

Friendly Letter

A **friendly letter** is a letter you write to someone you know.
A friendly letter has five parts. They are the heading, greeting, body,
closing, and signature.
Example:

heading —— October 22, 2003

greeting —— Dear Grandma,

body ——   The sweater you knitted for my birthday is great!
The fall days here have been chilly. It's nice to have a
new, warm sweater to wear. It is just the right size.
Thank you, Grandma.

closing —— Love,

signature —— Emily

How to Write a Friendly Letter
1. Choose a friend or a relative to write to.
2. Write about things you have done.
3. Be sure your letter has a heading, greeting, body,
   closing, and signature.
4. Use capital letters and commas correctly.

 **DIRECTIONS** > **Read the *Example* friendly letter. Answer the questions.**

1. Whom did Emily write the letter to?

_____

2. Why did Emily write the letter?

_____

Friendly Letter, page 2

Think of someone you want to write to. Use the organizer below to write your friendly letter.

heading _____

greeting _____

body _____

_____

_____

_____

_____

_____

_____

_____

_____

closing _____

signature _____

Envelopes

An **envelope** is used to send a letter or a note.
Example:

Mary Jo Wood
13 West Street
Chicago, Illinois 60648 — **return address**   **stamp**

Mrs. May Williams
13 River Bend Road
Crystal Lake, Illinois 60014 — **mailing address**

How to Address an Envelope
1. In the mailing address, tell who is receiving the letter.
2. In the return address, tell who is sending the letter.
3. Put a stamp on the envelope.

DIRECTIONS Think of someone you want to write to. Use the organizer below to address your envelope.

How-To Paragraph

In a **how-to paragraph**, a writer tells how to make or do something. The steps are told in order.

Example:

    Here is how to make a bird feeder. You will need a pine cone, string, peanut butter, and birdseed. First, tie the string to the top of the pine cone. Next, roll the pine cone in peanut butter. Then, roll the pine cone in birdseed. Last, go outside and tie the pine cone to a tree branch.

How to Write a How-To Paragraph
1. Write a sentence that tells what the paragraph is about.
2. Write a sentence that lists things you need.
3. Tell how to do something in order.
4. Use the words <u>first</u>, <u>next</u>, <u>then</u>, and <u>last</u>.

 **Read the *Example* how-to paragraph. Answer the questions.**

1. What does the paragraph tell how to do?

_____

_____

2. What materials are needed?

_____

_____

How-To Paragraph, page 2

_____ Next, fill the can with water.   _____ Here is how to water a plant.

_____ Last, water the plant.   _____ First, get a watering can.

DIRECTIONS Finish the chart. Use the chart to write a how-to paragraph.

My topic: _____
Materials needed: _____   _____   _____
Steps: 1. _____   2. _____   3. _____   4. _____

_____

_____

_____

_____

_____

Information Paragraph

In a paragraph that gives **information**, a writer gives facts and details about one topic.

Example:

      Many African American people celebrate Kwanzaa. It is a celebration of the customs and history of African American people. It is a gathering time for families, like Thanksgiving. The holiday is celebrated for seven days. It begins the day after Christmas. On each night of Kwanzaa, a candle is lit. Each candle stands for a rule to help people live their lives.

How to Write an Information Paragraph
1. Write a topic sentence. Tell who or what your paragraph is about.
2. Indent the first line.
3. Write detail sentences. Give interesting facts about the person, animal, place, or thing.

 **DIRECTIONS**   Read the *Example* information paragraph. Answer the questions.

1. What is the topic sentence of the information paragraph?

_____

_____

2. Write one detail sentence from the paragraph.

_____

_____

Information Paragraph, page 2

 Think about a topic you would like to write about. Complete the chart. Use the chart to write an information paragraph.

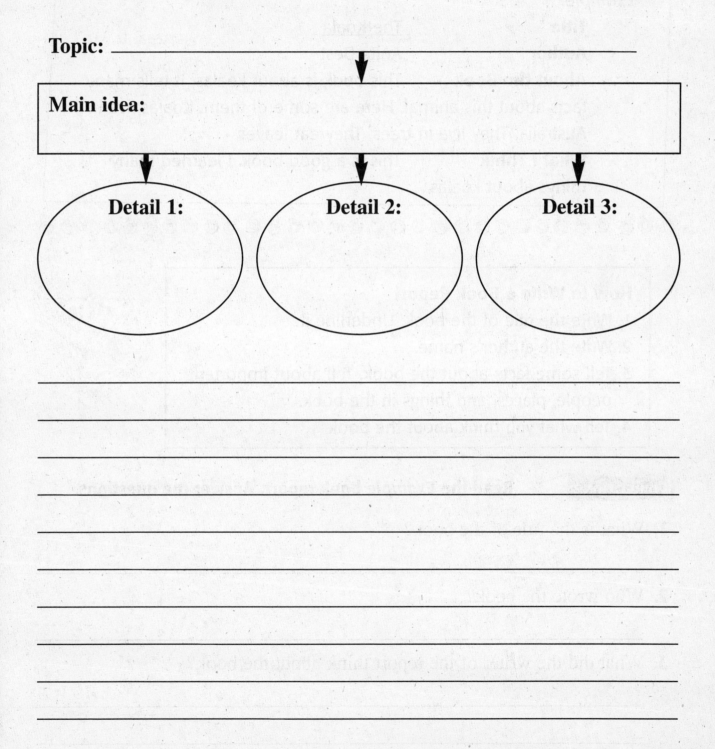

Topic: _____

Main idea:

Detail 1:

Detail 2:

Detail 3:

_____

_____

_____

_____

_____

_____

_____

_____

_____

Book Report

A **book report** tells about a book. It also tells what you think about the book.

Example:

Title	<u>The Koala</u>
Author	Anita Best
About the Book	This book is about koalas. It tells many facts about this animal. Here are some of them. Koalas live in Australia. They live in trees. They eat leaves.
What I Think	This is a good book. I learned many things about koalas.

How to Write a Book Report

1. Write the title of the book. Underline it.
2. Write the author's name.
3. Tell some facts about the book. Tell about important people, places, and things in the book.
4. Tell what you think about the book.

 **Read the *Example* book report. Answer the questions.**

1. What is the title of the book?

_____

2. Who wrote the book?

_____

3. What did the writer of the report think about the book?

_____

_____

Book Report, page 2

 **DIRECTIONS** Think of a book you would like to tell about. Fill in the information at the top and use it to write a book report.

Title of book: _____

Author of book: _____

Facts about book: _____

_____

_____

Should others read this book? _____

_____

_____

_____

_____

_____

_____

_____

_____

_____

_____

_____

Persuading Paragraph

A **persuading paragraph** tries to make the reader agree with the writer's opinion.
Example:

> I think that a lizard should be our class pet. A lizard is small and easy to care for. It doesn't eat much food. Lizards are interesting to watch, too. Vote for the lizard!

How to Write a Persuading Paragraph
1. Write about something you feel strongly about.
2. Tell how you feel in the first sentence.
3. Give reasons why other people should feel the same way.
4. Ask your reader to do something in the last sentence.

 **DIRECTIONS** Read the *Example* persuading paragraph. Answer the questions.

1. What is the writer's opinion in the first sentence?

_____

2. What is one reason the writer gives to make the reader agree?

_____

_____

3. What does the writer want the reader to do?

_____

_____

Persuading Paragraph, page 2

 Think of something you feel strongly about. Fill in the information at the top and use it to write a persuading paragraph.

Main idea: _____

Reason 1: _____

_____

Reason 2: _____

Reason 3 (your strongest reason): _____

_____

What the reader should do: _____

_____

_____

_____

_____

_____

_____

_____

_____

_____

_____

_____

Words in ABC Order

The order of letters from <u>A</u> to <u>Z</u> is called **ABC order**, or **alphabetical order**.

When words begin with the same letter, the next letter of the word is used to put the words in ABC order: <u>c</u>ape, <u>c</u>hapel, <u>c</u>ity.

DIRECTIONS ▷ **Number the words in ABC order. Then, write the words in the correct order.**

1. _____ bat   1. _____
   _____ air   2. _____
   _____ cat   3. _____

2. _____ top   1. _____
   _____ sea   2. _____
   _____ rock 3. _____

3. _____ egg   1. _____
   _____ fish 2. _____
   _____ dog   3. _____

4. _____ hat   1. _____
   _____ ice   2. _____
   _____ gate 3. _____

5. _____ joke 1. _____
   _____ lake 2. _____
   _____ king 3. _____

6. _____ neck 1. _____
   _____ owl   2. _____
   _____ mail 3. _____

7. _____ yes   1. _____
   _____ zoo   2. _____
   _____ walk 3. _____

8. _____ pan   1. _____
   _____ oak   2. _____
   _____ nail 3. _____

Using a Dictionary

A **dictionary** is a book that lists words and their meanings. The words in a dictionary are listed in ABC order.

Words can be put in ABC order. The first letters of these words were used to put them in ABC order.

<u>f</u>lower
<u>g</u>arden
<u>h</u>ome

Many words on a dictionary page begin with the same letter. When words begin with the same letter, the second letter is used to put the words in ABC order.

<u>se</u>eds
<u>st</u>ory
<u>su</u>n

DIRECTIONS Put each group of words in ABC order. Remember to use the second letter in each word if the first letter is the same.

1. noise _____
   music _____
   poem _____

2. sun _____
   rain _____
   plant _____

3. garden _____
   ground _____
   frog _____

4. afraid _____
   asleep _____
   alone _____

Using a Dictionary, page 2

Each word listed in the dictionary is called an **entry word**. Entry words are in ABC order.

The two words at the top of a dictionary page are called **guide words**. The word on the left is the first entry word on the page. The word on the right is the last entry word on the page. All the other entry words on the page are in ABC order between the first and the last words.

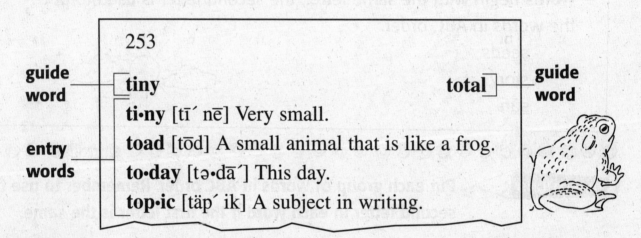

253

guide word — tiny   total — guide word

entry words —
ti·ny [tī´ nē] Very small.
toad [tōd] A small animal that is like a frog.
to·day [tə·dā´] This day.
top·ic [täp´ ik] A subject in writing.

▷ **DIRECTIONS**   Use the *Example* dictionary page. Answer these questions.

1. What is the first entry word on page 253? _____

2. Would you find the word <u>think</u> on this page? _____

3. What entry word tells about an animal? _____

4. What entry word means "very small"? _____

5. Could the entry word <u>together</u> be on this page? _____

Why or why not? _____

_____

Using a Dictionary, page 3

Some entry words have more than one meaning. Each meaning has a number.

The dictionary has sentences that show how to use the entry word.

bump [bump] **1** To knock against: The goblin <u>bumped</u> against the tree. **2** A part that sticks out: The goblin fell over a <u>bump</u> in the road.

burst [burst] **1** To break apart suddenly: The balloon <u>burst</u>. **2** To give way to a strong feeling: Grandfather and I <u>burst</u> into laughter.

 **Read the dictionary entries. Answer the questions.**

1. What word can mean "to break apart"? _____

2. What is the example sentence for meaning 2 of <u>burst</u>?

_____

3. Which word can mean "to knock against"?

_____

4. What is the number of the meaning of <u>bump</u> in this sentence?

The goblin fell over a <u>bump</u> in the road.

_____

5. Write your own example sentences for each meaning of <u>bump</u> and <u>burst</u>.

_____

_____

Using a Dictionary, page 4

 **DIRECTIONS** Use the dictionary words to answer the questions. Write <u>yes</u> or <u>no</u>.

always	at all times
animal	a living thing that is not a plant
bed	a place to sleep
dark	without light
green	the color of grass
hay	grass cut, dried, and used as food for cows and horses
hungry	needing food
kitten	a young cat
ladder	a set of steps used to climb up and down
library	a building where books are kept

1. Is <u>hay</u> something that alligators eat? _____

2. Is a <u>bed</u> a place for swimming? _____

3. Is grass <u>green</u>? _____

4. Is a flower an <u>animal</u>? _____

5. Can you use a <u>ladder</u> to climb to the roof? _____

6. Is a baby pig called a <u>kitten</u>? _____

7. Is a <u>library</u> a place for food? _____

8. Are you <u>hungry</u> after having lunch? _____

Using an Encyclopedia

An **encyclopedia** is a set of books that has facts on many subjects. Each book in a set is called a volume. The volumes list subjects in ABC order.

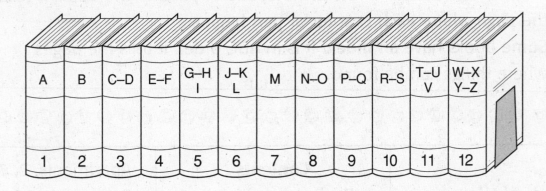

DIRECTIONS > Use the model encyclopedia in the picture. Write the number of the volume in which you would find each of these subjects.

1. Ohio River _____

2. explorers _____

3. Rocky Mountains _____

4. cows _____

5. United States _____

6. farming _____

DIRECTIONS > Write the word or words you would use to look up the following subjects in an encyclopedia.

7. pretty butterflies _____

8. kinds of dogs _____

9. trees in the United States _____

10. Florida history _____

Parts of a Book

The **title page** tells the title of a book. It gives the name of the author. The author is the person who wrote the book.

The **table of contents** lists the chapters or parts of the book. It tells the page where each chapter or part begins.

Some books have an **index**. It is in ABC order. It tells the pages where things can be found.

title page	table of contents	index
Kinds of Houses by Jack Builder	**Contents** 1. Brick Houses ....1 2. City Houses.................5 3. Country Houses.........8 4. Wood Houses..........15	Apartments, 2, 7 Basements, 25 Ceilings, 2, 9 Concrete, 4, 16 Doors, 12, 17

 **DIRECTIONS** Look at the sample pages. Answer these questions.

1. What is the title of the book? _____

2. Who wrote the book? _____

3. How many chapters are in this book? _____

4. On what page does chapter 4 begin? _____

5. On which pages can you find facts about ceilings? _____

Parts of a Book, page 2

The title page is in the front of a book. It tells you the title of the book. It tells you who wrote the book. It tells you who drew the pictures (illustrated) the book. And it tells you what company published the book.

DIRECTIONS **Look at this title page from a book about cats. Then, write your answers to the questions below on the lines.**

ALL ABOUT CATS
by
Patricia L. Keller

Illustrated by

Richard H. Green

Coaster Press
New York

1. What is the title of the book? _____

2. Who wrote the book? _____

3. Who illustrated the book? _____

4. What company published the book? _____

Parts of a Book, page 3

The table of contents is near the front of a book. It tells you what each chapter of the book is about. When you want to know what a book is about, you should read the table of contents.

 **DIRECTIONS** **Look at this page from the book <u>All About Cats</u>. Then, write the correct answers to the questions on the lines below.**

Table of Contents

CHAPTER	PAGE
1 Kinds of Cats	.3
2 Picking the Right Cat	.7
3 Taking Care of Your Cat	.12
4 Playing with Your Cat	.18
5 If Your Cat Gets Sick	.23
6 Cats in the Wild	.27

1. What chapter tells you what to do if your cat gets sick? _____

2. What chapter tells you about different kinds of cats? _____

3. What page tells you how to pick the right cat? _____

4. What is the name of the chapter on page 27?

_____

Kinds of Books

Some books are called **fiction**. They are stories about make-believe people and things. Here are some titles of books that are fiction.

     <u>Ask Mr. Bear</u>

     <u>The Bears Go to the Hospital</u>

Nonfiction books tell about real people or things. These books are nonfiction.

     <u>The Hospital Book</u>

     <u>Who Keeps Us Safe?</u>

A library has fiction and nonfiction books. The fiction books are in one part of the library. The nonfiction books are in another part.

○ ○○ ○○ ○○○ ○ ○○ ○○ ○ ○○○ ○○ ○ ○○ ○ ○○○ ○○ ○ ○○ ○○ ○

▌DIRECTIONS ▷ **Read about each book. Tell if the book is <u>fiction</u> or <u>nonfiction</u>.**

1. a book about a magic bear _____

2. a book that tells how to keep your home safe _____

3. a book that tells how to ride a bicycle safely _____

4. a book about a bear that can draw _____

5. a book about a house that can talk _____

6. a book about the fire department _____

7. a book about a dog that can fly _____

Fact or Fantasy?

Some stories that you read tell you facts about things. They tell you what could really happen. You might read about how a kitten likes to chase a mouse. This is really true. It is a **fact**.

Some stories tell about things that could not happen. In these stories, animals may talk or act like people. People may do things that could not really happen. These stories are called **fantasy**. "Goldilocks and the Three Bears" is a fantasy. It could not really happen.

DIRECTIONS **Read each sentence. Write <u>fact</u> by the sentences that are true. Write <u>fantasy</u> by the sentences that could not really happen.**

_____ **1.** Some elephants live in the jungle.

_____ **2.** The elephant read three books today.

_____ **3.** The pig built a brick house.

_____ **4.** That monkey grabbed my hat!

_____ **5.** The chicken put on an apron and washed the dishes.

_____ **6.** The oven said, "The cake is done."

_____ **7.** A zookeeper takes care of animals.

_____ **8.** Annie put on her magic ring and disappeared.

Core Skills: Language Arts, Grade 2

Answer Key

page 5
Order may vary. **1.** apple, **2.** bird, **3.** boy, **4.** car, **5.** chair, **6.** desk, **7.** girl, **8.** grass, **9.** pen, **10.** rug, **11.** tree, **12.** truck, **13.** girl, apple, **14.** bird, tree, **15.** chair, desk, **16.** boy, chair, **17.** girl, truck

page 6
1. sister, park, **2.** car, mother, **3.** dog, **4.** boy, birds, trees, **5.** playground, **6.** cat, slide; Chart: Person: sister, mother, boy; Place: park, playground; Thing: car, trees, slide; Animal: dog, birds, cat

page 7
Order may vary. **1.** Bob's Bikes, **2.** Bridge Road, **3.** China, **4.** Elf Corn, **5.** Gabriel, **6.** Lindsey, **7.** New York City, **8.** Oregon, **9.** Pat Green, **10.** State Street, **11.** Hill's Store, **12.** Baker Street, **13.** Stone Library, **14.** Emily Fuller

page 8
1. Where did Jack Sprat go?, **2.** Mary saw her friend Jill., **3.** Did Mr. or Mrs. Sprat go with them?, **4.** They met Ms. Muffet along the way., **5.–6.** Proper nouns will vary.

page 9
1. They walked along Main Street., **2.** My uncle drove through Indiana and Ohio., **3.** We went on a trip to Mexico., **4.–8.** Proper nouns will vary.

page 10
1. Wednesday, **2.** February, **3.** Saturday, **4.** Thanksgiving, **5.–7.** Answers will vary.

page 11
1. boys, **2.** girl, **3.** robe, **4.** stars, **5.** moon, **6.** house, **7.** door, **8.** treats, **9.** cats, **10.** dogs, **11.** owl, **12.** stars, **13.** trees, **14.** hands, **15.** song

page 12
1. caps, **2.** chairs, **3.** girls, **4.** trees, **5.** flags, **6.** boys, **7.** seeds, **8.** carrots, **9.** peas, **10.** friends, **11.** gardens

page 13
1. lunches, **2.** dresses, **3.** glasses, **4.** dishes, **5.** boxes, **6.** watches, **7.** foxes, **8.** benches, **9.** inches, **10.** brushes, **11.** buses, **12.** churches

page 14
1. woman, **2.** men, **3.** child, **4.** feet, **5.** teeth, **6.** children, **7.** feet, **8.** teeth, **9.** men, **10.** women

page 15
1. We, **2.** She or He, **3.** She or He, **4.** It, **5.** She or He, **6.** It, **7.** They, **8.** We, **9.** They, **10.** We

page 16
1. I, **2.** me, **3.** me, **4.** I, **5.** Susan and I, **6.** Tina and me, **7.** Tina and I, **8.** Susan and me

page 17
1. runs, **2.** kicks, **3.** breaks, **4.** looks, **5.** shakes, **6.** turns, **7.** runs, **8.** talks, **9.** sends, **10.** pays; **11.–15.** Answers may vary. **11.** The boy reads., **12.** The baby cries., **13.** The rabbit hops., **14.** The birds sing., **15.** The dogs bark.

page 18
1. skips, **2.** play, **3.** hug, **4.** purrs, **5.** barks, **6.** hide, **7.** waves, **8.** blows, **9.** follows, **10.** sees, **11.** hears, **12.** move, **13.** hoots, **14.** take, **15.** eat

page 19
1. have, **2.** have, **3.** had, **4.** has, **5.** has, **6.** has, **7.** have, **8.** had, **9.** has, **10.** have, **11.** have, **12.** had

page 20
1. are, **2.** are, **3.** were, **4.** is, **5.** are, **6.** were, **7.** is, **8.** am, **9.** was, **10.** is

page 21
1. plays, **2.** runs, **3.** dance, **4.** wait, **5.** leaps; Paragraph (Answers may vary.): takes, sits, asks, dances, stands, walks

page 22
1. played, **2.** visited, **3.** looked, **4.** jumped, **5.** leaned, **6.** helped, **7.** laughed, **8.** The girls played in the park., **9.** They climbed over rocks., **10.** Their fathers called to them.

page 23
1. ran, **2.** came, **3.** went, **4.** go, **5.** run, **6.** goes, **7.** goes, went, **8.** comes, came, **9.** come, came, **10.** run, ran

page 24
1. played, **2.** called, **3.** wanted, **4.** laughed, **5.** jumped, **6.** played, **7.** laughing, **8.** playing, **9.** talking, **10.** Carmen helped Grandma cook yesterday., **11.** Grandma is cooking some soup today.

page 25
1. are, **2.** is, **3.** are, **4.** is, **5.** are, **6.** are, **7.** are, **8.** are; **9.–10.** Sentences will vary.

page 26
1. were, **2.** was, **3.** were, **4.** were, **5.** were, **6.** was, **7.** was, **8.** were; **9.–10.** Sentences will vary.

page 27
1. sees, **2.** saw, **3.** sees, **4.** sees, **5.** saw, **6.** saw, **7.** see, **8.** saw, **9.** saw, **10.** see; **11.** saw; Last week we saw Lee., **12.** sees; Lee sees my painting now.

page 28
1. ran; Horses ran wild long ago., **2.** run; A horse can run ten miles every day., **3.** run; Can you run as fast as a horse?, **4.** ran; Mandy ran in a race last week., **5.** runs; Carl runs home from school now., **6.** runs; Now Mandy runs after Carl., **7.** run; How far can you run?

page 29
1. give, 2. gave, 3. gives, 4. gave, 5. gave, 6. gave,
7. gave, 8. gave, 9.–11. Sentences will vary.

page 30
1. do, 2. does, 3. does, 4. does, 5. does, 6. do, 7. does,
8. do, 9. does, 10. do, 11.–12. Sentences will vary.

page 31
1. had, 2. has, 3. have, 4. have, 5. has, 6. had, 7. has,
8. has, 9. have, 10. had, 11. had, 12. has

page 32
Answers may vary. 1. pink, 2. long, 3. brown, 4. round,
5. juicy, 6. tiny

page 33
Answers will vary. 1. tired, 2. happy, 3. many, 4. one,
5. hungry, 6. some, 7. three, 8. sleepy

page 34
2. brighter, 3. tallest, 4. fast, 5. thicker, 6. biggest,
7. wider, 8. oldest

page 35
1. an, 2. a, 3. a, 4. an, 5. a, 6. an, 7. an, 8. an, 9. a, 10. a,
11. an, 12. a, 13. an, 14. an, 15. a, 16. a, 17. a, 18. an,
19. an, 20. an, 21. a, 22. a

page 36
1. no, 2. yes, 3. no, 4. yes, 5. yes, 6. yes, 7. no, 8. no,
9. yes, 10. yes, 11. yes, 12. no, 13. yes, 14. no, 15. yes

page 37
Answers may vary. 1. Mrs. Brown lives on my street.,
2. Our building is made of wood., 3. Four families live in
our building., 4. Our class went on a picnic., 5. Jennifer
was climbing the tree., 6. The sun shone all day., 7. Corn
and beans grow on a farm., 8. The wagon has a broken
wheel., 9. The mother goat fed the baby goat., 10. The
boat sailed in strong winds., 11. The fisher caught seven
fish., 12. Some of the fish were sold in the store.,
13. Our team won ten games., 14. Our batters hit the ball
a lot., 15. The ballpark was full of fans., 16. Sentences
will vary.

page 38
Answers will vary.

page 39
The following parts of each sentence should be circled:
1. My family and I, 2. Sami Harper, 3. Miss Jenkins,
4. Mr. Chang, 5. Henry, 6. Mr. Byrne, 7. Mrs. Lee,
8. Mr. and Mrs. Diaz, 9. Jeanine, 10. Mr. Wolf, 11. Amy
Taft, 12. Mr. Dowd, 13. Mrs. Clark, 14. Carolyn and
Alberto, 15. Julie

page 40
1. fly, 2. buzz, 3. barks, 4. quack, 5. hops, 6. roar,
7. moo, 8. cluck; Sentences will vary.

page 41
1. My brother eats apples., 2. Elizabeth drinks milk.,
3. Kim likes peanut butter., 4. Justin wants bread.,
5. Chris plants corn., 6. Chang caught a fish., 7. Dad
cooks breakfast., 8. Shawn shares his lunch., 9. Rosa
grew the carrot.

page 42
1. telling, 2. telling, 3. asking, 4. not a sentence,
5. telling, 6. not a sentence, 7. telling, 8. asking,
9. telling

page 43
1. statement, 2. question, 3. statement, 4. question,
5. statement, 6. question, 7. exclamation, 8. statement,
9. question, 10. exclamation

page 44
Sentences will vary. Be sure each sentence is the
specified kind.

page 45
1. John gave seeds to Sara and told her to plant them.,
2. Sara planted the seeds and looked at the ground.,
3. Sara sang songs and read stories to her seeds.,
4. The rain fell on the seeds and helped them grow.

page 46
1. The farmer and his family stood in the doorway.,
2. The hunter and the bear stayed with the family.,
3. The mice and the children ran out the door.,
4. The hunter and the bear went home.

page 47
Answers will vary. Be sure each new sentence contains
describing words.

page 48
1. The ant climbed down a blade of grass. He (or She)
fell into the spring., 2. The bird pulled off a leaf. He (or
She) let it fall into the water., 3. The hunter saw a lion.
He (or She) spread his net., 4. The lion and I live in the
woods. We are friends.

page 49
Answers will vary. Possible responses: 1. stroll, 2. race,
3. pedal, 4. speed, 5. zooms, 6. jogs, 7. skip, 8. travels,
9. sails

page 50
1. Mark Twain, 2. Beverly Cleary, 3. Diane Dillon,
4. Alicia Acker, 5. Ezra Jack Keats; The first letter of
these words should be circled: 6. mother, grandma,
7. grandma, grandpa, 8. uncle carlos, aunt kathy,
9. Mario Martinez told me a story., 10. Ichiro and I
played ball.

page 51
1. C.D., 2. C.A.C., 3. M.B., 4. M.T., 5. K.S., 6. T.L.T.,
7. I.B., 8. C.L.W., 9. J.W.A., 10. L.B. Hopkins, 11. A.
Martinez, 12. Patricia A. Rosen, 13. The box was for
M.S. Mills., 14. D.E. Ellis sent it to her., 15. T.J. Lee
brought the box to the house.

page 52
1. Mrs. Ruth Scott, 2. Mr. Kurt Wiese, 3. Miss E. Garcia, 4. Dr. Seuss, 5. Ms. Carol Baylor, 6. Mr. and Mrs. H. Cox, 7. Miss K.E. Jones, 8. Dr. S. Tomas Rios, 9. Mrs. H. Stone is here to see Dr. Brooks., 10. Mr. F. Green and Ms. Miller are not here.

page 53
1. James lives in Dayton, Ohio., 2. His house is on Market St., 3. I think Thomas Park is in this town., 4. We went to Mathis Lake for a picnic. 5. Is Parker School far away?

page 54
1. Monday, 2. Friday, 3. February, 4. Answers will vary., 5. November, 6. Tues., 7. Thurs., 8. Dec., 9. Sat., 10. Jan., 11. Sept.

page 55
1. New Year's Day, 2. Mother's Day, 3. Independence Day, 4. Labor Day, 5. Cinco de Mayo, 6. Thanksgiving Day, 7. Veterans Day, 8. Earth Day is in April., 9. Boxing Day is a British holiday., 10. Father's Day is in June.

page 56
1. Best Friends, 2. The Biggest Bear, 3. Rabbits on Roller Skates, 4. Down on the Sunny Farm; The first letter of these words should be circled: 5. we, bees, 6. the, dancing, pony, 7. my, shadow, 8. my, summer, farm

page 57
The first letter in each sentence should be capitalized.

page 58
1. Patty played on the baseball team., 2. Patty hit two home runs., 3. She caught the ball, too., 4. What time is it?, 5. Is it time for lunch?, 6. Are you ready to eat?

page 59
1.–5. Each sentence should end with a period., 6. Ms., 7. Mr., 8. Mrs., 9. Dr., 10. Ms.

page 60
1. !, 2. ?, 3. ?, 4. !, 5. don't, 6. I'll, 7. didn't

page 61
1. were not, weren't, 2. was not, wasn't, 3. has not, hasn't, 4. have not, haven't, 5. did not, didn't, 6. are not, aren't, 7. is not, 8. do not, 9. was not, 10. can not, 11. did not, 12. had not, 13. does not, 14. are not, 15. isn't, 16. don't, 17. didn't

page 62
June 8, 2003 / Dear Grandmother, / The tag says it comes from Chicago, Illinois. / Love,

page 63
1. Akron, Ohio, 2. Hilo, Hawaii, 3. Macon, Georgia, 4. Nome, Alaska, 5. Provo, Utah, 6. Nancy lives in Barnet, Vermont., 7. Mr. Hill went to Houston, Texas., 8. Did Bruce like Bend, Oregon?, 9. Will Amy visit Newark, Ohio?, 10. How far away is Salem, Maine?

page 64
1. Dec. 12, 1948, 2. Mar. 27, 1965, 3. Sept. 8, 1994, 4. Nov. 1, 2000, 5. Jan. 5, 1995, 6. August 10, 1967, 7. Oct. 17, 1983, 8. February 8, 1991, 9. July 29, 1989, 10. Sept. 3, 2001, 11. Oct. 20, 1988, 12. Answers will vary.

page 65
1. hat, 2. bee, 3. cow, 4. dog

page 66
1. road, 2. home, 3. sad, 4. sick, 5. gift, 6. small, 7. large, 8. dog, 9. yell, 10. great, 11. dad, 12. sleep

page 67
1. soft, 2. long, 3. dark, 4. on, 5. happy, 6. low, 7. dry, 8. slow, 9. bad, 10. cold, 11. go, 12. hard

page 68
1. a, 2. b, 3. a, 4. a, 5. a, 6. b, 7. a, 8. b, 9. a, 10. a, 11. b, 12. a

page 69
1. hear, 2. here, 3. here, 4. hear, 5. You're, 6. your, 7. you're, 8. your

page 70
1. write, 2. right, 3. right, 4. write, 5. right, 6. write, 7. right, 8. right, 9. write, 10. right

page 71
1. to, 2. two, 3. to, 4. to, 5. too, 6. two, 7. too, 8. too, 9. to, 10. to, 11. two

page 72
1. their, 2. They're, 3. there, 4. their, 5. there, 6. They're, 7. They're, 8. there, 9. there, 10. Their, 11. there, 12. They're

page 73
1. sunglasses, 2. afternoon, 3. playground, 4. birthday, 5. outside, 6. scrapbook, 7. sunglasses, 8. afternoon, 9. scrapbook, 10. birthday, 11. outside, 12. playground

page 74
1. unable; not able, 2. reopened; opened again, 3. unlucky; not lucky, 4. unfair; not fair, 5. unhappy; not happy, 6. rewind; wind again, 7. rewashed; washed again, 8. uneven; not even, 9. refilled; filled again, 10. reknitted; knitted again

page 75

1. careful; full of care, 2. harmless; without harm,
3. breakable; able to be broken, 4. dreadful; full of dread,
5. hopeful; full of hope, 6. thankful; full of thanks

page 76

Answers will vary.

page 77

Answers will vary. Sentences should be about school
safety.

page 78

1. Uncle Joe is a funny man., 2. Dad told us a funny
story about his dog., 3. Firefighters are brave people.

page 79

The first sentence in each paragraph should be circled.
The other sentences should be underlined.

page 80

Top: 3, 2, 4, 1; Bottom: 2, 3, 4, 1

page 81

1. The story takes place at the zoo., 2. They watch the
monkeys play., 3. They feed the seals.

page 82

Answers will vary.

page 83

1. The poem is about things the writer likes., 2. Answers
will vary: bows, rose, toes, nose., 3. Answers will vary:
white, blue, sweet, red, crunchy, wet, black.

page 84

Answers will vary.

page 85

1. birds in the writer's backyard., 2. red, tiny, sweetly,
buzz, 3. Sentences will vary. Be sure that the sentence
supports the topic.

page 86

Answers will vary.

page 87

1. her grandmother, 2. to thank her grandmother

page 89

Check that the envelope is filled in correctly.

page 90

1. how to make a bird feeder, 2. a pine cone, string,
peanut butter, and birdseed

page 91

Order of steps: 3, 4, 1, 2

page 92

1. Many African American people celebrate Kwanzaa.,
2. Answers will vary but should be any sentence in the
paragraph except the first.

page 94

1. The Koala, 2. Anita Best, 3. that it is a good book

page 96

1. that a lizard should be the class pet, 2. Answers will
vary. A lizard is small and easy to care for. A lizard
doesn't eat much food. A lizard is interesting to watch.,
3. vote for the lizard

page 97

Reports will vary.

page 98

1. 2, 1, 3; air, bat, cat, 2. 3, 2, 1; rock, sea, top, 3. 2, 3, 1;
dog, egg, fish, 4. 2, 3, 1; gate, hat, ice, 5. 1, 3, 2; joke,
king, lake, 6. 2, 3, 1; mail, neck, owl, 7. 2, 3, 1; walk,
yes, zoo; 8. 3, 2, 1; nail, oak, pan

page 99

1. music, noise, poem, 2. plant, rain, sun, 3. frog, garden,
ground, 4. afraid, alone, asleep

page 100

1. tiny, 2. no, 3. toad, 4. tiny, 5. yes, because the word
together falls between tiny and total in ABC order.

page 101

1. burst, 2. Grandfather and I burst into laughter.,
3. bump, 4. 2, 5. Answers will vary; examples: I have a
bump on my head., The water pipe burst.

page 102

1. no, 2. no, 3. yes, 4. no, 5. yes, 6. no, 7. no, 8. no

page 103

1. 8, 2. 4, 3. 10, 4. 3, 5. 11, 6. 4, 7. butterflies, 8. dogs,
9. trees or United States, 10. history, Florida

page 104

1. Kinds of Houses, 2. Jack Builder, 3. 4, 4. page 15,
5. 2, 9

page 105

1. All About Cats, 2. Patricia L. Keller, 3. Richard H.
Green, 4. Coaster Press

page 106

1. 5, 2. 1, 3. 7, 4. "Cats in the Wild"

page 107

1. fiction, 2. nonfiction, 3. nonfiction, 4. fiction,
5. fiction, 6. nonfiction, 7. fiction

page 108

1. fact, 2. fantasy, 3. fantasy, 4. fact, 5. fantasy,
6. fantasy, 7. fact, 8. fantasy